THE CONCEPT OF HINDU NATION

THE CONCEPT OF HINDU NATION

ABHAS CHATTERJEE

VOICE OF INDIA
NEW DELHI

First published, 1995
First reprint, 2003
Second reprint, 2018

ISBN 81-85990-33-6

Published by Voice of India, 2/18, Ansari Road, New Delhi – 110 002.
Printed at D.K Fine Art Press (P) Ltd New Delhi-110052

Contents

The Concept of Hindu Nation*

Over the last few years, the terms 'Hindutva' and 'Hindu Rashtra' have been very much in the air. Specially so between 1988 — when the Ramajanmabhumi liberation movement started gathering momentum — and 1993, when the Bharatiya Janata Party suffered serious electoral reverses in the mid-term elections in U.P. and other north Indian States. During these years, Hindutva and Hindu Rashtra appeared to figure prominently all around — in our news columns and editorials, in the lectures of our political leaders, in the manifestoes and statements of political parties. Be it in support or in virulent opposition, everyone was seriously expressing views on Hindutva and Hindu Rashtra, which terms persistently dominated all discussions during these years.

Some Prevalent Misconceptions

But, in spite of all this discussion, it has never been made clear as to what the term 'Hindu Rashtra' really means. Notwithstanding all the speeches, editorials and articles, some basic confusion continues to prevail regarding the meaning of Hindu Rashtra or the Hindu Nation.

We come across futuristic statements like 'we shall make a Hindu Nation (Rashtra)', or 'no one can prevent the formation of the Hindu Nation', or 'a Hindu Nation can never be created', and so on. Such statements obviously imply that no Hindu Nation has been in existence so far. But if that be so, how does one talk at the same time about the national honour

* Revised and expanded version of a lecture delivered on 31 July 1994 at Mahajati Sadan, Calcutta, under the auspices of Purvanchal Kalyan Ashram and Friends of Tribal Society.

(*asmitā*) of the Hindus?

In some public meetings addressed by a prominent political personage of our country, a gentleman who is regarded by most people as a champion of Hindu Rashtra, an enthusiastic audience raised the slogan, 'He alone will rule over this country who stands by the Hindu cause.' The leader lost no time in prohibiting this slogan and told the audience, 'Please say that he alone will rule over the country who abides by the nation's cause.' This obviously implied that the terms 'Hindu' and 'the nation' are not identical. But if so, then how does the same leader speaks of the Hindu Rashtra?

Any number of leaders considered to be supporters of the Hindu Rashtra keep repeating that there is nothing basically wrong with the Indian Constitution as framed at present; nothing wrong, they say, with the concept of Secularism either; only some aberrations have arisen in the system on account of appeasement of the minorities, and so we are opposed, they say, to this policy of appeasement. Well, if that be so, will the Hindu Rashtra come into being merely by doing away with these policies of appeasement?

To me all this confusion appears to be quite unwarranted. As far as I have been able to understand, the concept of Hindu Nation or Hindu Rashtra is extremely simple. It can really be spelt out in mere five words, and these five words are: WE HINDUS ARE A NATION. Please mark my words again: "We Hindus are a nation." In 1946, when the Muslim League's demand for partition of India and creation of a separate state of Pakistan was being seriously debated, someone asked M.A. Jinnah, "You keep talking of Pakistan. Could you explain what is your concept of this Pakistan? What do you really mean by it?" Jinnah replied, "Of course. In just five words." Then he uttered those five famous words: "We Muslims are a nation." And he went on to elaborate his thesis of cultural difference, incompatibility, and impossibility of co-existence with Hindus, and so on. I do have some strong reservation on the point whether Mohammedans of undivided India indeed constituted a separate nation. But I have not an iota of doubt that the counterpart of that idea, namely, that we Hindus are a nation, is hundred per cent true. We Hindus are not just a religious community like the Mohammedans and the Christians but a nation unto ourselves. The term 'Hindu' is the name of our nationality. "We Hindus are a nation" — this is a basic, simple and undisputable truth. Unfortunately, even this simple truth we are unable to appreciate, and that failure lies at the root of all our misconceptions and miseries.

What is A Nation?

Our misconception has arisen from the fact that we have not tried to comprehend the definition of a nation. We normally take a nation to stand for a country, a landmass, a specific portion of the globe. But a nation never means a land as such. A nation indicates a group or community of people which has been traditionally living in a particular land, which has its own distinctive culture, and which has an identity separate from other peoples of the world by virtue of the distinctiveness of its culture. The cultural distinctiveness of a nation may be based on its race, or religion, or language, or a combination of some or all of these factors, but all-in-all there has to be a distinct culture which will mark the nation out from peoples belonging to other lands. Third, there may be internal differences in several respects among the people belonging to this culture, but in spite of these differences there is an overall sense of harmony born out of the fundamental elements of their culture, and a sense of pride which inspires in them a desire to maintain their separate identity from the rest of the world. Finally, as a result of these factors, this group of people has its own outlook towards the history of its traditional homeland; it has its own heroes and villains, its own view of glory and shame, success and failure, victory and defeat.

A community of people which possesses the above features is a NATION, and the country in which it has been traditionally living, and where it has developed its distinct culture, is called the MOTHERLAND of that nation, its TRADITIONAL HOMELAND. But the country or the land by itself can never be the nation. In other words, a nation is not a territorial unit but an emotional unit with a territorial base. As Sri Aurobindo had said, "A nation is indeed the outward expression of a community of sentiments whether it be the sentiment of a common blood, or the sentiment of a common religion, or the sentiment of a common interest, or any or all of these sentiments combined."

Once we start looking at things from this viewpoint; we immediately see not only that we Hindus are a nation unto ourselves, but also that we are the oldest surviving nation on earth. The distinctiveness of the Hindu culture gives us a markedly separate identity quite apart from the rest of the world. And the distinctive culture of our nation is the Sanātana Dharma. This Sanātana Dharma has any number of branches and offshoots. Within its fold, we have the Vaidika and the Tantrika, the Buddhist and the Jain; we have the Shaiva and the Vaishnava, the Shakta and the Sikh, the Arya Samaj and the Kabirpanth; we have in its fold the worshippers of Ayappa in Kerala, of Sarna in Chotonagpur and of Doni-pollo in Arunachal Pradesh. There are, in fact, an immense number of forms and variations of the vast vision of Sanātana Dharma, but through all these forms and variations flows an underlying current of shared spirituality which makes us all Hindus and gives us an intrinsic sense of harmony.

There are many points of difference within the Hindu fold, caused by caste, language and regional tradition. But the fundamental sense of Hindu identity, unity, and harmony cuts through all differences and prevails over the community on account of the common spiritual current of the Sanātana Dharma. Thus it is the Sanātana Dharma which is the distinguishing feature of the Hindu nation.

Hindus and their Homeland

The traditional homeland of Hindus is the Bhāratavarsha. It is a quite distinct geographical entity. There are few nations in the world the natural boundaries of whose homeland are as clearly drawn as that of ours. Mother Nature has herself created and bequeathed to us, as it were, the separate land of Bhāratavarsha enclosed by the Himalayas and the Hindukush, the Indian Ocean, the Arab Sea and the Bay of Bengal. It appears as if Nature, or the Supreme Being if you like, has specially created this country as the motherland of a particular nation. And the Hindus have been intimately associated with this land, lived on it, developed their culture and civilization on it, and regarded it as sacred soil, for at least 6000 years if not many more.

Of course, when I say Bhāratavarsha in the sense of the Motherland of the Hindus, it must be kept in mind that I do not refer to the boundaries of the truncated India that we have today, but to those of our traditional homeland which extends continuously from Gandhar to Kamrup and from Kashmir to Kanyakumari.

This basically is the concept of Hindu nationhood, or what we call Hindutva or Hindu Rashtra.

The one bitter truth that we have to acknowledge in this context is that we remained subjugated for about a thousand years when foreign invaders ruled over our country. By use of barbaric persecution or economic inducements, they compelled certain segments of our nation to abandon their ancestral culture and adopt the culture of those foreign invaders. More tragically, after a few generations passed, these hapless people forgot that the culture they had adopted was a foreign culture, a culture that belonged to another nation and had been forced on them. They started regarding the alien culture as their own, developed an affinity with it, and identified themselves with it. Foreign domination thus led to the twin misfortune of our losing control over some parts of our traditional homeland, and some segments of our nation getting fractured away from the rest of us.

But subjugation does not by itself destroy the nationhood of a nation. Nor does the nature of the nation, the basic characteristic and disposition of the nation, get changed by the fact of enslavement. Nations do get destroyed. There are situations in which a nation gets obliterated, its national distinctiveness gets wiped out. But subjugation of a nation by itself does not imply its destruction or change of its character. The two are not synonymous. A nation may live through and well survive long spells of slavery.

We Hindus are a nation just as the Germans are a nation, the Armenians are a nation, the Kurds are a nation, the Jews are a nation. Look at the German nation. Their traditional homeland was divided into two. But this did not abate their nationhood. Within a mere fifty years, they achieved re-unification of their homeland and the nation was restored to its original complexion. As for the Jewish nation, they had in fact completely lost hold of their motherland. For nearly 2000 years, they remained separated from their traditional homeland. But even that did not cause extinction of the nationhood of the Jews. The Jews remained a nation and despite so much of persecution and tyranny, they re-established their own state in their traditional homeland after 2000 years. The Hindus too have remained a nation, no matter who managed to rule over our homeland during the last millenium. The quintessence of the nation has remained intact. Its substance and entity have remained intact.

The Perception of Swami Vivekananda

That 'we Hindus are a nation' is by no means a new idea. This idea has been with us for a long time, in fact throughout our history. I am not tracing it back very far, and will confine myself to modern times. If you read Swami Dayananda Saraswati, you will come across the notion that we Hindus are a nation. In the writings of Bankimchandra and Sri Aurobindo too, you will find a clear and confident assertion that we Hindus are a nation, and not just a religious community. The basic perception of Vir Savarkar was also the same which he forcefully presented in his famous book, *Hindutva*. However, the person who made the most powerful pronouncement of this idea was Swami Vivekananda. Throughout his brief but momentous life, Swamiji proclaimed — loudly, clearly and consistently — the fact that we Hindus are a nation.

I would like to remind you of the brief 5-minute first address of Swamiji delivered at the inaugural session of the Parliament of Religions at Chicago. In that address Swamiji told his American audience, "I thank you in the name of the millions and millions of Hindu people of all classes and sects." Thereafter he spoke three sentences which were most significant. First, he said, "I am proud to belong to *a religion* which has taught the world both tolerance and universal acceptance." Next, he said, "I am proud to belong to *a nation* which has sheltered the persecuted and the refugees of all religions and all nations of the earth." He cited an example, namely, that when the sacred temple of the Jews had been demolished by the Romans, we Hindus gave shelter to the Jewish refugees and took care of them. In the third sentence, Swamiji said, "I am proud to belong to *the religion* which has sheltered and is still fostering the remnants of the grand Zoroastrian nation."

Thus, in three consecutive sentences Swamiji proclaimed his pride of belonging first "to a religion", then "to a nation", and again "to a religion."[1]

1. Sri Aurobindo spoke in identical terms in 1909 when he received the message in the communion of Yoga during his stay in the Alipore Jail: "It is *this religion* that I am raising before the world, it is this that I have perfected and developed through the Rishis, saints and Avatars, and now it is arising forth to do my work among the nations. I am raising up *this nation* to send forth my word."

There is absolutely no doubt that Swamiji used the words 'religion' and 'nation' as synonymous. For him there was no difference between the two, It is also abundantly clear as to which 'religion' or 'nation' he was talking about, and what his perception of nationhood was.

In the writings and speeches of Swami Vivekananda, we come across hundreds of references to the reawakening of the Hindu nation, the resurgence of the Hindu nation, and the rejuvenation of the Hindu nation. Indeed, regeneration of the Hindu nation was the central theme of his thought. One finds his writings full of expressions such as 'the national vision of the Hindus', 'the national traditions of the Hindus'. He keeps referring to the national glory and destiny of the Hindus, their national ethos and history, their national consciousness and goal. He speaks of the national literature of the Hindus, their national characteristics, their national backbone and efficiency. He talks of the Hindu national edifice and *raison d'etre* of the Hindu nation, the national task for the Hindus and the ship of the Hindu nation. In fact, all his writings, speeches, and interviews are literally strewn with expressions like these.

Swamiji is also emphatically clear that the essential feature of Hindu nationhood is the Hindu religion, the Sanātana Dharma.

At one place, he says that in spite of the slavery of a thousand years and tyranny of centuries, the Hindu nation is still alive because it did not forsake the basic element of its national life, namely, the Dharma. By Dharma here he means the Sanātana Dharma only. Elsewhere he says that Sanātana Dharma itself is our national life. In yet another place he asserts that the Hindu nation still survives because no one could destroy its soul, viz. Sanātana Dharma. He asserts that Sanātana Dharma is our distinctive feature. It is only we Hindus who, in the history of the world, never invaded the land of any other nation. On one occasion he says that the quintessence of the Hindu national life is spirituality, that we Hindus have to keep this national ideal of ours above everything else, and that if we give up spirituality we would be destroyed as a nation.[2]

'*Ekam sad viprāh bahudhā vadanti*' is a message, said Swamiji, that has entered the blood-stream of the Hindu nation. He pointed out that foreign aggressions destroyed thousands of our temples but they all came up again because this is our national life-current. Swamiji contrasted the Hindus with other nations by saying that the national goal of the French was political liberty, of the British mercantile genius, and of the Hindus spirituality. On one occasion, Swamiji went to the extent of claiming that of all the nations of the world, Hindus are the most handsome, and he added "I am not saying this because I belong to that nation, but because this is the truth."

It is thus evident that Swami Vivekananda had a clear vision and had made a forthright proclamation, at the turn of the century, of the basic theme (*mūlamantra*) that we Hindus are a nation, and that the distinctive feature of our nationhood is Sanātana Dharma.

That we Hindus are a nation unto ourselves and not just a religious community — this cardinal truth formed the basic plank of our first national movement in this century, viz. the Swadeshi Movement. When Bengal was partitioned in 1905, the entire Hindu society rose up with a national inspiration. No one had the slightest doubt at that time that we Hindus are a nation. That is why in this very city of

2. For Sri Aurobindo too India was identical with the Sanātana Dharma. In his famous Uttarpara Speech in 1909, he said, "When therefore it is said that India shall rise, it is the Sanātan Dharma that shall rise. When it is said that India shall be great, it is the Sanātan Dharma that shall be great. When it is said that India shall expand and extend itself, it is the Sanātan Dharma that shall expand and extend itself over the world. It is for the Dharma and by the Dharma that India exists... I say that it is the Sanātan Dharma which for us is nationalism."

Calcutta, gatherings of 50,000 people took a collective oath before Goddess Kali in the holy Kalighat temple that we shall throw the British out of our homeland. Numbers touching 50,000 marched through the streets after taking a dip in the holy Ganges, anointing their foreheads with *tilak*, and holding copies of the Bhagvad Gita in their hands. No one saw any difference in those days between Sanātana Dharma and Indian nationalism. There was a clarity of thought, namely, that Sanātana Dharma is the distinguishing feature of the Indian nation.

An Alternate Perception: 'The *Bhāratīya* Nation'

However, an alternate perception of the nation was introduced in the country shortly afterwards. As the Mohammedans, egged on by their British patron, kept raising their demands — and backed them by the standard Islamic weapon of violence — the soft Hindu leaders sought the softer option. Instead of facing Islamic hooliganism squarely, they tried to accommodate its practitioners. And in their anxiety, they sought to redefine our nationhood. They started to deny that we Hindus have been a nation since ancient times, and proclaimed instead that India was still a 'nation in the making', that the Indian nation will rise out of coalescence of Hindus and Muslims. This was nothing short of self-deception. And this new approach gave rise to an alternate concept of the Indian nation by 1920. Knowingly or unknowingly, it was Mahatma Gandhi who became the architect of this new concept, although he had great faith in Sanātana Dharma. Of the major mistakes that he committed during his leadership, the most serious was his attempt to take Mohammedans along in our national movement. This attempt at an impossibility — it failed ultimately as it was doomed to do — led him to lay the foundation of a new concept of the nation in India. Inspired by Gandhiji or from other motives, some other leaders also started promoting this concept. Finally, as Pandit Jawaharlal Nehru came to dominate the political scene more and more, he promoted this falsehood and made this alternate concept strike its roots wider and deeper.

The alternate concept is simply this: all those who happens to reside on the soil of India together form a nation. According to this concept, every resident of the country — whether one follows the culture of this country or has adopted some alien culture, whether one is loyal to this country or not, whatever be one's attitude towards the heritage of this country, no matter if one even regards the culture of this country as abominable and a path of the Devil — all such persons are still be agglomerated to form one nation.

This new concept of the nation was also given a new name — *Bhāratīya*. The new concept thus bade good-bye to the cardinal principles of nationhood, viz. emotional unity, and all that it implies. It turned the nation into a geographical entity, although the truth is that a nation is never a mere geographical entity and that a nation remains a nation even if it loses inhabitance of its traditional homeland.

So, according to the alternate perception, Hindus are not a nation but a mere religious community, just as the Mohammedans are a community, the Christians are a community, and so on. And all these communities put together are supposed to constitute the '*Bhāratīya*' nation. Thus, in the Gandhi-Nehru era the meaning of the words 'India' and 'Indian' was changed, and we Hindus were reduced from the status of a nation to that of a religious community only, a mere part of 'the nation'.

It is evident that both of these alternative perceptions cannot be valid at the same time. It is for you to judge which perception is right and which is wrong.

But this was not the end of the matter. This new concept of a geographical or composite nation — which Jawaharlal

Nehru used all his power and prestige to propagate since 1947 so as to implant it in the Hindu psyche — had some significant implications. These implications formed the corner-stone of all policies of the Nehru era and proved disastrous for Hindus.

The first implication was that Hindus being the largest community, it was potentially dangerous for the other communities. Secondly, since this community posed a potential threat to the other communities, the more it could be weakened the better it would be for the health of the nation. Third, the good of the other communities was also the national good because their participation constituted the crucial element of our nationhood.

Therefore, the theory went, "Make the Hindu community as weak as you can, by creating internal divisions in it, by denigrating its culture, by inflicting insults on it, and by whatever other means you can afford." I am sure I do not have to enumerate before this audience the various efforts that have been made during the last 50 years to weaken us Hindus in pursuance of this theory. With a little reflection, you will be able to recall them all.

Fourth, in keeping with the new concept, a new idea called *sarva-dharma-samabhāva* was propagated. It suggested that since our 'nation' was constituted by an assemblage of several religious communities, we should regard the ideology or religion of every community as India's national heritage and hold them all in equal respect. That is, we should yield the same place to the Koran and the Bible in our thinking as we do for the Bhagvad Gita. We should have the same reverence for Mohammed and Jesus as we have for Sri Rama, Sri Krishna and Bhagvan Buddha. We should accept Mohammed and Jesus also as part of our national pantheon and conduct ourselves accordingly. The idea of regarding alien cultures also as our own thus gained currency through the convenient slogan of *sarva-dharma-samabhāva*.

Fifth, since the distinctiveness of the largest community was Sanātana Dharma, it was necessary — we were made to believe — for the good of other communities to run down the Sanātana Dharma as well. As far as possible, therefore, condemn the whole of Hindu culture — Hinduism is nothing more than a bunch of superstitions and castes and idolatries, the whole of Sanātana Dharma rests on myths, this is not a progressive religion, and so on. A cult of denigrating the Sanātana Dharma was promoted, directly or indirectly, by these and many other similar calumnies.

Finally, we were taught to look at the history of Bhāratavarsha from a new angle of vision. We were asked to regard India's history as one of synthesis. We were asked to overlook the barbaric tyranny that was perpetrated on us in order to force Islam down our throat. The horrible persecution, the plunder, the vandalism, and the massacres should all be forgotten. Or we should assume these to have been the personal aberrations of a few rulers. In order to project the history of India as a history of synthesis, an imaginary course of events was constructed, viz. that from olden days foreigners kept on coming to India and settling down by and by, that they kept getting mingled with one another and a new 'nation' was thus formed, a new culture was thus created. So, we don't really have a national culture of our own, but only a composite culture.

In this alternate concept of nationhood, according to which Hindus are no more than a religious community and all inhabitants of India together constitute one nation, the most important element, therefore, was opposition to Hindus. In fact, antagonism to Hindus emerged as the single most distinctive feature of this perception, because promotion of what was perceived under it as the 'national interest' pre-supposed supplanting of Hindu interests. Since the most important role in spreading this concept was played by the thoughts and actions of Jawaharlal Nehru, you could name this theory or ideology as Nehruism. In course of time this very ideology came to be lauded, acclaimed, promoted, and propagated under the name 'Secularism' till it came to be treated beyond reproach, beyond debate and discussion.

How deep was Nehru's faith in and commitment to this ideology would be evident from several of his statements. In 1949, addressing a meeting in Farrukhabad, Nehru had said that to talk of the Hindu culture would injure India's interests. While delivering a lecture at the Lucknow University in 1951, he said, "The ideology of Hindu Dharma is completely out of tune with the present times and if it took root in India, it would smash the country to pieces." In a letter to Kailash Nath Katju in 1953, he wrote, "In practice, the individual (Hindu) is more intolerant and more narrow-minded than almost any person in any other country." In fact, as early as 1947 itself, Nehru had proudly proclaimed in a public meeting, "As long as I am at the helm of affairs, India will not become a Hindu State." You of course know that speaking about himself Nehru had once stated that by education he was an Englishman, by views an internationalist, by culture a Muslim, and a Hindu only by accident of birth. With all this evidence, there is little scope for doubt that Nehru had a deep contempt for Hindu religion, for Hindu culture, for Hindu society, and for the average Hindu.

Truth versus Falsehood

Thus we have before us two alternate perceptions of our nation — one of Swami Vivekananda and other of Jawaharlal Nehru. One says that Hindu Dharma is the quintessence of your national life, hold fast to it if you want your country to survive, or else you would be wiped out in three generations. The other, coming a mere 50 years later, tells us that if the Hindu Dharma thrives, the country will be smashed to pieces. One says that Hindu culture is the life-current of our nation, the other says it would injure the nation even to talk of Hindu culture. Swamiji went around telling the whole world that if any people has a proven record of tolerance it is the Hindus, but Nehru thinks the Hindus to be the most intolerant in the world. Swamiji is emphatic that India can once again attain the pinnacle of glory in the comity of nations through the power of Hindu Dharma and Hindu culture, whereas Nehru believes that Hindu Dharma and culture are totally out of place in the present age. One was supremely proud of being a Hindu, the other so ashamed of it as to reject it as an accident of birth.

Obviously, both these perceptions cannot be right. It is for us to judge as to which of the two is telling the truth and which the lie.

It is a tragedy that, since 1947, the alternate perception of Indian nationalism — the Nehruvian perception — has got embedded in the public mind. You may yourself judge if there is even an iota of truth in this perception. Mahatma Gandhi, as I have said, was the founding father of this perception in the real sense, but even the life-long tireless efforts of such a saintly figure could not translate the perception into reality. After 30 years of ceaseless endeavour, the Mahatma failed miserably in all he had worked for and Pakistan was created. This single event proved conclusively that the perception of a 'composite' Indian nation was no more than a figment of his imagination. I have no doubt whatsoever that the concept of a 'composite' Indian nation that has been propagated in our midst during the Gandhi-Nehru era, the concept which has provided the guideline for running the polity of this country for the last 50 years, is an imaginary nation. It is a concept based on wishful thinking, built on a fiction. No such nation ever existed in the past, none exists at present, and none is likely to exist in future.

Composite Culture: A Myth

The allied concept of a 'composite *Bhāratīya* culture' is equally imaginary. The fact is that the national culture of India is the Hindu culture. The remnants of some other cultures left behind on our soil by foreign invaders and rulers also exist side by side. Aggressor cultures have left similar remnants in many other countries of the world. This does not mean a demise of the national culture or creation of some 'composite' culture. On the contrary, the aggressor culture is always regarded as an enemy culture or a parasite culture. It remains the constant endeavour of every nation to discard that culture as far as possible and not allow its national culture to be polluted by it. In the days of the Ottoman Empire, the Turks foisted their culture for four long centuries on Bulgaria and forcibly converted many Bulgarians to Islam. But the Bulgarians do not regard their culture as 'composite'. Rather, after gaining independence, their national State totally repudiated the Islamic culture, even to the extent of forbidding people from using Islamic names. Muslims held Spain under their sway for 500 years and imposed Islamic culture on it. But when the Spaniards threw them out under the Reconquesta campaign, they took care to obliterate even the last vestiges of the Moorish (or Islamic) culture from their land. They did not consider their own culture to have become 'composite'; rather they prohibited the practice of Islam on their soil.

The purpose of promoting the concept of composite culture in India is simple — it is that we should accept Islamic (and to some extent Christian) culture also to be our own culture, a part of our own heritage. The reality, however, is just the reverse. Even after a thousand years of co-existence, Hindu and Islamic cultures have not only remained parallel cultures but have also come in conflict on every conceivable point. In matters physical or spiritual, of principle or of practice, on every point sublime or trivial, the two cultures have remained as unblended as oil and water. Islamic culture was brought to this country by barbaric invaders and tried relentlessly for a thousand years to extirpate the national Hindu culture. For us, therefore, it is nothing short of an enemy culture, a parasite culture.

It is also a bitter truth that there are fundamental differences between the two cultures; their premises and ethos are so antithetical to each other that they can never become composite in any foreseeable future.

After the tremendous growth of science and technology, there could scarcely be a country in the world which has not undergone some cultural interaction with other countries and where one would not find fragments of certain alien cultures. But this does not destroy the character and substance of the national culture. Some Muslims in India have taken to Hindu music, or Muslim rulers have left some buildings, or innate religious liberalism has inspired some Hindus to pay obeisance to the tombs of Muslim fakirs at some places — all this can hardly make our national culture composite. Yet this is the fare on which we have fed our 'Secularism'.

Composite Culture: the Islamic Perception

There is hardly any novelty in this viewpoint either. Please look at the views of all the Muslim theologians of India from the 18th century onwards. Shah Waliullah in the 18th century, Shariatullah, Syed Ahmad Barelvi, Abdul Aziz, Titu Mir etc. in the 19th century, and Mohammad Iqbal, Maulana Maudoodi and others in the 20th — all of them have said what I am saying today. None of these worthies ever accepted that Muslims and Hindus of India together make one nation or that our culture is a composite one. All of them emphasized that in India Muslims have a separate nationality (*qaum, awām*) and a separate culture. And frankly, if you ask me, had I been a Muslim, I too would have never accepted that my nationality and culture are the same as yours. Because the Koran itself firmly rejects such an idea. As per the Koran, the Muslims by themselves constitute a separate nation, the *Ummah*. A person within the fold of *kufr* can never be a part of the *Ummah*. *Kāfirs*, the practitioners of *kufr*, are also of two categories in the eyes of Islam — the *Zimmīs* and the *Mushriks*. Jews and Christians who are *Kitābīs* (i.e. people with a revealed book) are regarded as *Zimmīs*. They can live in an Islamic state provided they pay the poll-tax (*jizyah*) and renounce all public life. Twenty degrading conditions are imposed on them in exchange for the favour of the right to live. These conditions reduce them to third or fourth grade citizens. But at least the right to life is granted to the *Zimmīs*. But for the *Mushriks* which means idol-worshippers, the only choice is between Islam and death.

As per the Koran, we Hindus come under this category of *Mushriks*, whom that 'holy' book does not even grant the right to live. The Koran does not permit its adherents to live peacefully as equal citizens with the *Kāfirs* in any country. For the *Mushriks,* the Koran gives only two options — either they convert to Islam, or their men be slain and their women, children and properties be taken over as rightful plunder. According to the Koran this land of ours is a *Jāhiliyyah*, a land of darkness. It will remain a *Jāhiliyyah* till the rule of Islam is fully established here. Muslims believe the Koran to be words of Allah himself, and as adherents to the Koran they have no freedom to believe that in the present stage of history, when India is still predominantly Hindu, they are a part of the Indian nation.

The Hadis gives even clearer instructions, namely, that if Muslims are compelled to live in a *Jāhiliyyah*, their foremost duty is to wage war and slaughter the *Kāfirs* so as to conquer the land and establish Islam there. If such conquest is not possible at present, Muslims should bide time and continue to build their strength. In case that too appears impossible to achieve, then Muslims should leave that country and migrate elsewhere. This migration is called the *Hijrah*. So, the Hadis tells the Muslims, "Perform the *Hijrah* if necessary, but never concede becoming part of a *Mushrik* nation." If any Muslim really considers himself to be a part of this nation on the basis of equality with you and me, he would be doing so only by an implicit repudiation of the Koran and the Hadis, by violating a basic tenet of Islam, by straying away from the cardinal principles laid down for a true Mohammedan.

Therefore, the concept of a composite nation combining Hindus and Muslims is false to its very core. But the affairs of our State have been conducted since 1947 entirely on the basis of this false perception of nationality. To sustain this fundamental untruth, the system here has to take recourse to other untruths on every conceivable issue. Bangladeshi Muslims are infiltrating into Assam, Bengal, Bihar and other parts of India in millions, but you cannot say that the infiltrators are Muslim. In Kashmir, Muslims have waged what is avowedly a *Jihād* and tyrannised the entire Hindu population out of the Valley, but you have to say that the strife in Kashmir is not communal, it is a battle for *Kāshmīriyat*! Muslims carried out devastating bomb explosions in Bombay and Calcutta, but you have to say that this was the handiwork of Pakistanis or underworld dons. Muslims start communal riots ever so often. You have to say that there was a clash "between two groups of people" and avoid mentioning as to who started the carnage. Muslims burn temples. You have to say that the "place of worship of a particular community was damaged". Muslims are breeding faster than others. But you have to ignore this easily recognizable fact.

It seems to me that all our national weaknesses and problems today spring from this basic mischief. The artificial vision of nationality on which our system is functioning is quite different from our real nationality. The grave consequence of the basic dichotomy has been a complete evaporation of national inspiration in the country. A Hindu of post-1947 India has great difficulty in feeling himself to be a part of the imaginary nation for which the whole system is being operated. He is unable to identify himself emotionally with that imaginary, artificial, 'composite' national entity which the Indian State has been representing. An enormous gulf has thus been created between the Nation and the State, between the national society and the ruling class. It is this gulf which is causing disintegration of the national society, disappearance of collective consciousness and sensitivity, degeneration of social conscience. It is because of this hiatus that selfishness, corruption and moral degradation have proliferated fast. The national society has been alienated from the State and the national will to face problems has all but vanished.

The False Perception gains Currency

Tragically, it is this false Nehruvian vision which today dominates the minds of the ruling elite of this country. It is the concept of a geographical nation that pervades the minds of our intelligentsia, our politicians, editors of our newspapers. The vicious propaganda carried on for 50 years has created such a situation that our intelligentsia today sincerely believes that Hindus are only a religious community, and therefore, whoever talks of Hindus talks only about a community, and is therefore 'communal'. What is evidently national to us appears communal to them. They have drunk so deep of the poison of Nehruvian thought that the alternate perception of nationality has been deeply ingrained in their minds, and quite possibly they consider people like me honestly to be 'communal'.

The situation is so bad that even Swami Vivekananda's thoughts are today interpreted from the viewpoint of Nehruism. A distorted vision of Swamiji's message is being presented in order to create the impression that Swamiji's ideas about the nation were the same as those of Nehru who came later. The sayings of Swamiji are presented in a manner that one would think Swamiji to have said the same thing that Nehru did later. In fact, the views of Nehru are being projected in the name of Swamiji.

In reality, however, Hindu religion, Hindu nation, Hindu race and India, all these four terms are synonymous and interchangeable in all writings of Swami Vivekananda, from beginning to end. At many places, Swamiji used the words 'Hindu' and 'India' in identical sense in the same sentence. To illustrate this point, may I read out to you a very famous paragraph of Swamiji's article, 'Modern India'? In it, Swamiji had written:

> Oh India! Forget not that the ideal of thy womanhood is Sita, Savitri, Damayanti; forget not that the God thou worshippest is the great ascetic of ascetics, the all-renouncing Umanath Shankara; forget not that thy marriage, thy wealth, thy life are not for sense-pleasure, are not for thy individual personal happiness; forget not that thou art born as a sacrifice to the Mother's altar; forget not that thy social order is but the reflex of the infinite Mahamaya; forget not that the lower classes, the ignorant, the poor, the illiterate, the cobbler, the sweeper, are thy flesh and blood, thy brothers. Thou brave one, be bold, take courage, be pround that thou art an Indian (*Bhāratavāsī*), and proudly proclaim, "I am an Indian, every Indian is my brother. Say, the ignorant Indian, the poor and destitute Indian, the Brahmin Indian, the Pariah Indian is my brother." Thou, too, clad with a rag round thy loins proudly proclaim at the top of thy voice: "The Indian is my brother, the Indian is my life. India's gods and goddesses are my God. India's society is the cradle of my infancy, the pleasure-garden of my youth, the sacred heaven, the Varanasi of my old age." Say brother: "The soil of India is my highest heaven, the good of India is my good," and repeat and pray day and night, "O Gaurinath, O Jagdambe, bestow manliness unto

me! O thou Mother of Strength, take away my weakness, take away my unmanliness, and make me a Man!"

In this message, Swamiji used the word "India (*Bhārata*)" five times and "Indian (*Bhāratavāsī*)" eight times. But please mark whom he was addressing by these words. "The ideal of thy womanhood," he said, "is Sita, Savitri, Damayanti", but which is that India, who are those Indian women who regard Sita, Savitri and Damayanti to be their ideal? They are not the Indians of Nehruvian fantasy, but Hindu women only. When Swamiji said that "the God thou worshippest is... Umanath Shankara", he was talking to Hindus only. When he said that "thou art born as a sacrifice to the Mother's altar", could he be addressing a Muslim or a Christian to whom the very idea of offering a sacrifice to the Mother is utterly repugnant? He said that the lower classes, the ignorant, the poor, the cobbler and the sweeper are your brothers. He did not say the Hindu and the Muslim, but the cobbler and the sweeper; he was clearly speaking of the two weakest and most helpless segments of the Hindu society only. In saying "Brahmin Indian and Pariah Indian" again, he was obviously addressing the Hindu society at the two ends of which stand the Brahmin and the Pariah. Which is the nation that would accept that Gods and Goddesses of India are my God? India's society, he said, "is my sacred heaven, the Varanasi of my old age", but who are the people to whom Varanasi is the holiest abode? Who are the people that consider the "soil of India my highest heaven", and not a *Jāhiliyyah* or *Dar-ul-harb*? Who are the Indians that address their prayers to Gaurinath and Jagdambe?

This message of Swamiji is addressed, word by word, to Hindus and to none else. But he uses the words "India (*Bhārata*)" and "Indian (*Bhāratavāsī*)" because for him the three words — Hindu, India, Indian — are synonymous. You would, however, notice that these days huge hoardings are put up in which it is written: "Proudly proclaim, 'I am an Indian and every Indian is my brother' — Swami Vivekananda." This tearing of words from their context is clearly an attempt to spread the false notion among the general public that Swamiji had also used the word "*Bhāratavāsī*" with the same connotation that Nehru later put in the word "*Bhāratīya*" and the one that is being promoted by the State media since 1947 — viz. a mere geographic Indian. I have written several letters to the Ramakrishna Mission asking why they are distorting Swamiji's message so as to put Nehru's words into Swamiji's mouth. But there is no satisfactory reply. The nation-perception of Nehru is being publicized today in the name of Swamiji, although Swamiji's vision of the nation was totally different.

The situation is so bad that even people like us who talk about the Hindu nation appear to have internalized, at least partially, the Secularist perception. We speak of the Hindu nation in meetings such as the present one today, but, when we go out, we do not call ourselves Hindu. Whenever we have to indicate our nationality, we declare ourselves as *Bhāratīya* or Indian. Many of you here are often staying in hotels. In the guest registers of the hotels, you have to fill up your name, address and nationality. If my impression is right, all of you here, my friends, must be writing 'Indian' in the column of your nationality, not Hindu. Please tell me, is there anyone amongst you here who declares his nationality to be Hindu? The prevalent meaning of the word '*Bhāratīya*' or 'Indian' today is the same as Nehru's though that is only a fictitious nationality. When we declare ourselves as *Bhāratīya* or Indian, we would be naturally interpreted to have called ourselves so in the Secularist sense.

Recently, I had to open a fresh bank account. So, in the appropriate form, I wrote 'Hindu' in the column meant for nationality. The bank manager objected that one has to mention one's nationality in that column, not religion. I told him that my nationality was Hindu. He said that as per the circulars of the Reserve Bank of India (RBI), he could not accept my form. I replied, "That's too bad. I don't know what the RBI circular says. But I am a Hindu and can proclaim my nationality to be Hindu and nothing else. I can't possibly change my nationality in deference to the RBI circular. If you can't open my account because of this, please don't bother; I won't open the account. But I consider my nationality to be Hindu and cannot compromise on that point." Anyway, the manager was kind enough to open my account after all.

If we really have the faith that we Hindus are a nation, then we should forthwith drop our adherence to the Nehruvian myth of a composite nation and start acting everywhere in accordance with our own perception. You have to write your nationality in the disembarkation cards of airflights, but probably there too you have been declaring yourself not to be 'Hindus' but 'Indians'. If nothing else, could we not start immediately proclaiming our nationality as Hindu in, say, hotels, international flights, application forms for students, various forms to apply for jobs, financial investments and so on?

The Geographic Concept of 'Hindu'

Some people would like to define every inhabitant of Hindusthan as a Hindu. This idea which was initiated by Sir Syed Ahmed Khan in 1884, is wrong and misleading. It is an attempt to characterize Hindus as a geographical expression instead of as a cultural-national entity. This idea makes the name 'Hindu' bear the same meaning as '*Bhāratīya*' of the Nehruvians. As per this definition, even persons like Abdullah Bukhari, Syed Shahabuddin and Ibrahim Memon would qualify to be called Hindus. Such a notion would not only be ridiculous but also insulting to

Hindutva. The distinctive feature of *Hindutva*, as we noted earlier, is the Sanātana Dharma. Only a follower of this great and glorious spiritual tradition, in any of its myriad forms, is a Hindu, and no one else. Quite possibly, it was some aliens of yore who first called our country Hind, and us Hindus. But even at that time, this name carried with it the connotation of the culture of Sanātana Dharma. Later on, when we adopted this name for ourselves, we held this name to represent our cultural-national identity; we felt proud of our being Hindus. For centuries on end, we fought many battles to protect and preserve our *Hindutva*, made enormous sacrifices and suffered unspeakable oppression to save our identity as Hindus. Therefore, we must avoid falling into the trap of robbing the word 'Hindu' of its cultural underpinnings and giving it a purely geographical meaning.

The Concept of a Minority

A question would naturally arise in your mind in this context, namely, that if we Hindus are a nation unto ourselves, what would be the status of Muslims and Christians living in this country? Are they not a part of this nation? Some people even raise the question: Are we going to throw them out of the country? The simple answer to this question is that there is difference between being a part of a nation and the citizen of a state. A person may not be a part of a nation although he may be a citizen of its state, and it is such a person who is truly characterized as a minority. Indeed, this is the correct concept of a minority. India is the homeland of the Hindu nation; so, the residents of this land who have alienated themselves from her national attribute — Sanātana Dharma — are no more part of this nation, but minorities. They may be granted citizenship of our State and all rights of a citizen, but they would remain minorities, rather than being 'nationals' of our land.

All over the world, inhabitants of a country are in fact

classified in these two categories — nationals and minorities. It is only in India that a wrong notion has been introduced of having two classes, a majority and a minority, *within* the rank of nationals. As a matter of fact, when a fragment of one nation happens to be living, for reasons historical or geographical, in the traditional homeland of another nation, or when its own homeland is annexed by another nation, this segment of population becomes a minority in that country. A few examples will make the idea clear. In China, the Tibetans whose language, religion and race are different from the Chinese — Han — people are regarded as a minority. In Bangladesh, Hindus who are distinguished only by a different religion are considered a minority. In Canada, it is the French-speaking people of Quebec who are treated as a minority. Bulgaria regards as her minority the Muslim Turks whose religion and race and language are different from those of the Bulgars. In USA, it is the Blacks who are regarded as a minority because of their different race.

Evidently, the yardstick of identifying a minority is religion in one place, language in another, race in yet another, and a combination of two or more factors in still another. Why should this be so? This is because the distinctiveness which accounts for a segmental population's failure to become a part of the nation of the country, the distinctiveness which fixes their basic national loyalty to some other land, the distinctiveness which prevents them to share the national sentiments of the nation — that distinctive factor becomes the basis of marking out the segment as a minority in that country.

It is also not essential that all members of a nation should always live in their own homeland. Indian followers of Sanātana Dharma are parts of the Hindu nation. Many of them have gone to the U.S.A., obtained the Green Card, and become citizens of that State, but they still continue to remain members of the Hindu nation, and will remain so till they lose their attachment to Sanātana Dharma and the soil of Bhāratavarsha. Many Tibetans have been living in India but they continue to remain nationals of the Tibetan nation. Jews may have settled down in India or in Argentina, but they continue to be parts of the Jewish nation.

Muslims and Christians: Minorities or Nationals?

With that background in mind, it is necessary to remember an important fact about the Muslims and the Christians of India, namely, that they are our own people. Till only a few generations ago they were parts of our nation. But the persecutions and allurements of the alien rulers compelled them to accept an alien culture and they themselves developed, in course of time, a sense of alienation from their own ancestral culture. The only wall that stands between them and us is this alien culture. Demolish this wall of Islam or Christianity and there would be nothing to separate the Indian Muslims and Indian Christians from the rest of us.

The relation between our minorities and the alien cultures they have adopted is that of a patient with his disease. We do not consider an ailing family member to be our enemy; rather we try to terminate his disease so that he may be cured and live a happy, harmonious life with other members of the family as before. Probably a still more apt comparison of the relationship would be with that between the drug and the drug-addict. A drug-addict develops such intense attachment to his favourite drug that it becomes the thing closest to his heart; he cannot even imagine his life without it. But we know how deadly a poison the drug is for him. It becomes our definite objective, our sacred duty, to de-addict our kin from the fatal influence of the drug.

We ought not, therefore, have any animosity towards the Muslims and the Christians of India. Our enmity, our fight, has to be against those baneful ideologies — Islam and Christianity — which have created, in the minds of some of our own people, a hostility against their original culture, which have alienated them from the culture of their own ancestors, and created in them a loyalty for some alien lands. Our objective has to be to rescue these strayed members of our nation from their addiction to alien ideologies, and restore them to the national mainstream. We have to finish Islam from this country, not Muslims.

It is not necessary, however, that every Indian Muslim or Indian Christian would be outside the pale of the Hindu nation. The nationality of each one of them would depend on his or her personal attitude. Mere acceptance of a foreign mode of worship cannot exclude a person from the Hindu nation, because Sanātana Dharma permits complete freedom as regards mode of worship. The mere fact that someone wishes to venerate a formless (*nirākāra*) God instead of an image (*sākāra*), or likes to offer prayers facing the west, or regards Fridays or Sundays as special days for obeisance, or fasts for a month during the day, or regards Jesus Christ as his favourite deity (*īshṭadeva*), would not put a person outside the fold of our nation. This much latitude Sanātana Dharma certainly gives us. Even an atheist is regarded in our ethos as a Hindu, so why cannot a worshipper of Allah or Jesus remain a Hindu?

The crux of the problem lies in believing or not believing the theologies of these religions. A Muslim who actually believe in the theology of Islam can never be a member of the Hindu nation. Those who believe, in accordance with that theology, that Sanātana Dharma is obnoxious, that our ancestors were misguided people, that our *rishis* and *munis* were followers of the Devil, that all our ancestors have their places reserved in hell, that on the day of *qiyamat* (the last judgment) we too can only expect to be consigned to the fires of hell and never see the doors of heaven; those who believe that all our Gods and Goddesses and Avatāras are false abominations, that we are committing cardinal sin by worshipping them, that the alien ideology adopted by them is the only right path and true religion, that India is a *Jāhiliyyah* waiting to be redeemed, that Allah himself has decreed it to be an act of great virtue (*kār-i-sabāb*) to slaughter, plunder and torture the Hindus — such people can by no means be a part of the Hindu nation.

The basic notes of Christian theology are not very different from that of Islam, but considerable liberalism now sweeps across the Christian societies of the world so that, by and large, it has ceased to be important for the Christians now to really believe in their theology. We can, therefore, find a large number of persons among Christians of India — and we may also find a few Muslims of that class — who may be following the modes of worship of alien religions, but who have retained a reverence for Sanātana Dharma, a sentiment for the culture of their ancestors, a cognition in their minds of the nationality of Hindus, and an emotional bond with its distinctive feature. Such persons continue to be parts of the Hindu nation in spite of adopting Christianity or Islam But persons who really believe in Islamic or Christian theology can only be a minority on the soil of our motherland, not nationals of it. It is, therefore, indisputable that most of the Muslims of present-day India are minorities, not nationals of our country.

As I said earlier, the accepted norm of classifying people in all countries and international institutions of the world is to see them as the nation and its minorities. That is why minorities are also referred to as sub-nationalities or sub-national minorities. Everywhere you would find only these two categories — the nation, and those who are unable to harmonise with it in spite of living on its soil, viz. the minorities. But in India the false and artificial nation-perception has created an altogether new concept, namely, that though every resident is a part of the nation, but some are minorities as well. That there should be 'a majority' and 'a minority' *within* the fold of the nation — this division is totally wrong.

Israel is the land of the Jewish nation. It has a seven per cent Arab population who are Muslims. In India, Muslims are 11% of the population, not very much more than in Israel. In Israel too, these Arabs have been granted full rights of a citizen, full freedom also to follow their religion. But they are regarded as a minority, not as part of the Jewish nation. It is not considered necessary to consult these Arabs on how the affairs of the Jewish nation would be conducted. We too need some clarity of thought as to what would be the political role of the people who are not within the pale of the Hindu nation. Their status can be that of minorities only, not of nationals. We would need to form a realistic assessment of their viewpoint, we would have to recognize their attitudes and aspirations on the basis of realism.

Hindus: A Nation but Not Yet Free

The significant point that merits most attention today is that though we Hindus are a nation, we are not yet an independent nation. We are still a subjugated nation. You would appreciate if you reflect a little seriously that on 15 August 1947, the Hindu nation did not actually gain freedom. Rather they underwent only a change of the master, a change of rulers. In 1757, after the Battle of Plassey, the British became our rulers instead of Muslims. Did that mean we had gained freedom then? Similarly, in 1947 though the British had to quit, the Hindu nation could not get the ruling power in its own hands because the new rulers who have came to power neither believe that Hindus are a nation nor consider themselves as part of the Hindu nation.

The plain but harsh truth is that in August 1947, the Muslim 'nation' of undivided India gained freedom, but not so the Hindus. The Muslims got recognition as a separate nation and a separate territory was carved out as their national homeland. They established their own state in that territory, and that state is still conducting its affairs by holding the cultural aspirations, honour and interests of the Muslims of Bhāratavarsha as its responsibility. But Hindus neither gained recognition as a nation, nor their own State, nor control over their national homeland.

You may ask: how are we not independent when India is being ruled by her own people? But the mere rule by persons belonging to the country does not make a nation independent. Idi Amin belonged to Uganda, but were the Ugandans free in his regime? In theUSSR under Stalin and Rumania under Ceausescu, those countries were under the reign of rulers hailing from their own countries, but were these nations free?

You may point out that these rulers were all dictators whereas in India we have democracy, we have the right here to change our government through elections. But so long as the electoral contest is limited to elements that deny the nationhood of the nation they are seeking to rule, elections are no indication of the nation's freedom. There used to be elections in the Soviet Union too, but the contest was limited to more than one candidate from within the Communist Party. Similarly, in India, Nehruism, or — what is the same thing — Secularism, has been made so sacred that no one rejecting that ideology can successfully fight elections at present. As clarified earlier, the essence of this Secularism is anti-Hinduism, and if any candidate today openly declares that he considers Hindus to be a nation, that he wishes to save the Hindus and fight for their interests, that he aims at freedom of the Hindus and seeks their support, his right to be elected stands forfeited. Even if he succeeds in the polls, the courts will declare his election null and void on the ground of 'communal publicity'. There are already examples of this in constituencies like Ville

Parle in Bombay. Therefore, in present-day India, our rights are limited to choosing our representatives from among candidates who subscribe to the ideology of Nehruism or Secularism or anti-Hinduism. And this is the ideology that guides all Secularist, Socialist, Communist and Islamist political parties in India, albeit with shades of variation here and there.

But as the cardinal principle of Secularism — or Nehruism — is anti-Hinduism and denial of Hindu nationhood, and as adherents to that ideology have willingly estranged themselves from the Hindu nation, it is clearly foolish for Hindus to regard such persons as Hindus and consider themselves to be independent and self-ruling after handing over state power into their hands.

An individual loses his identity when he adopts an antipodal ideology. Take any example. Shri Prayag Ram, the grandfather of the celebrated Mr. M.J. Akbar, was a Hindu, but he bestowed his faith on Islam; so he ceased to be a Hindu. Rev. Krishna Mohan Banerjee was a Hindu, but he adopted the creed of Christianity and ceased to be a Hindu. Lenin and Stalin had been both born in Christian families and were duly baptised, but once they became believers in Marxism, they could no longer be considered to be Christians. Similarly, a person who starts believing in Nehruvian Secularism — or Marxism for that matter — which is founded on antagonism to Hindu nationhood, cannot be logically considered to remain a Hindu, or a part of our nation. Nehruism is to the Hindu society what Marxism was to the Christians in Europe.

We mistakenly think the Secularists — or Nehruvians — also to be Hindus. Probably this confusion is caused by the fact that the Secularists have also adopted a few traditions, rituals and oblatory practices of the Hindu nation e.g. offering garlands on *samādhis* and portraits, paying emotionally reverent tributes, lighting lamps, occasionally having *darshana* of a saint or visiting a shrine, and so on. By these clever gimmicks they manage to befool us. Otherwise, people who have been ruling this country since 1947 are totally anti-Hindu and antagonists of Hindu nationhood, although they have adopted a few superficial Hindu customs. It is wrong to consider them Hindus or to regard their regime as self-rule by the Hindu.

Constitutional Discrimination

In case you do not find this theoretical analysis clear or convincing, you may well look at the practical aspect. The first hallmark of an independent nation is that it would have its own state, and would be recognized by other countries as a nation. Its state has to run its affairs in accordance with the aspirations, ethos, ideals and culture of the nation, represents the nation before the outside world, promotes the image of the nation and welfare of its members, and spreads the glory of its national culture. Such a state would create consciousness of national honour, national pride and national heritage in the young and old generations; it would be a state which would never permit the rights and status of its nationals to be inferior to those of any minorities, aliens and non-nationals. But none of these characteristics hold good for the Hindus in India after 1947.

Forget about other countries, the Indian State itself has not yet recognized Hindus as a nation. And since the state power in India has itself never taken any such initiative, the question of other countries recognising Hindus as a nation does not arise at all.

Second, the Indian Constitution has in effect given less rights to the Hindus than to the minorities in several matters. Under Article 30 of the Constitution, minorities have got the most precious right of running educational institutions in accordance with their own cultures and values, but Hindus have been denied this right. This discrimination means that the Indian State is more liberal in helping propagation of alien cultures than the promotion of Hindu culture. You cannot find such a perverse provision in the constitution of any independent nation of the world.

The right of 'propagation' of one's religion that has been bestowed by Article 25 of the Constitution on followers of different religions also means, for all practical purposes, that the adherents of alien and anti-Hindu religions will be at liberty to convert any follower of Hinduism — even if he be a minor — to their own creed.

In Article 51A, Hindu culture has not been accepted as India's national culture. Instead, it has been clearly stated that India's culture is a hotch-potch 'composite' culture. This means that we have to regard Islamic culture also as our own culture and to view with reverence even such enemies of the nation as Aurangzeb and Tipu Sultan.

In whichever state of India a non-Hindu community is numerically predominant, there the state government has been granted special rights under the Indian Constitution. You are all aware, I'm sure, about the Article 370 applicable to the State of Jammu & Kashmir. Similar special provisions have been made applicable to Nagaland under Article 371A and Mizoram under article 371G which provide that laws made by India's Parliament would not be applicable to these states unless their own state legislatures endorse them. That is, a state would have greater autonomy where the legislatures have preponderance of the minorities and where the government is in the hands of the minorities. No such autonomy is available to states where Hindus predominate.

Leave other things alone, even the Preamble of the Indian Constitution does not contain any Hindu idea. It enumerates no principles based on Hindu ethos and ideals. The Preamble talks of justice, equality, fraternity, and liberty as its goals. They may be good ideas in themselves, but what is the inspiration behind them? All of them are Western notions borrowed directly from the French Revolution. The national ideas of India, that is, of the Hindu nation, are — as Swami Vivekananda repeatedly reminded us — *dharma* and spirituality, renunciation and service, tolerance and harmony: *satyam vada, dharmam chara* (speak the truth, abide by *dharma)* — is the basal theme of our nation. But the present Indian Constitution has not incorporated a single idea out of these.

Anti-Hindu Policies and Laws

Let us proceed from the Constitution to the laws of the land and policies of the State. In almost all states of India, public undertakings styled as Minorities Finance Corporation have been formed. The Central Government is also proposing now to set up a similar undertaking by providing Rs. 500 crores as its initial capital.[3] These Corporations provide loans to people below a certain level of income and help them set up their own enterprises. But there is a condition. A person would be entitled to get the loan only if he is not a Hindu! You may be a learned yet destitute Hindu, a starving Hindu today struggling to earn a penny, but you cannot be financed. Get converted tomorrow to Islam or Christianity, and you will get the loan![4]

Article 32 of the Constitution has made a provision for protection of fundamental rights of all citizens through the judiciary. But the Central Government, and in their territories several State Governments, have passed a Minorities Commission Act to make a special arrangement for the protection of rights of those who are not Hindus. The Commissions that have been formed in pursuance of these laws grant representation to followers of alien creeds, but not to a Hindu, that is, to a follower of Sanātana Dharma who wishes to call himself a Hindu. It appears that the Hindus neither need solution of their social problems, nor the protection of their

3. The proposal has since been put into effect.
4. Hindus are entitled only to pay taxes for fattening the 'minority' communities.

collective community rights.

You are aware of a Muslim group in Kerala called the Moplahs. The only contribution of these people in the Freedom Movement was that, during the Khilafat agitation of 1921, they carried out a brutal massacre of Hindus in Malabar. They plundered thousands of Hindu homes and burnt Hindu villages, they raped Hindu women and destroyed Hindu temples. But you know what? Such of those Moplahs as are still alive are honoured by the Government of India as 'freedom fighters' and given monthly pension on that basis! The Moplahs are not known to have fought the British on any other occasion.

Is there a single independent nation in the world which does not have the right to sing its national song in its own Parliament? But in India, *Vande Mātaram* which we have recognized as our national song, was not allowed to be sung in the Parliament because some Muslim members objected to it!

Every free nation or state, no matter how small or weak it may be, protects — or at least attempts to protect — its own international borders against entry of aliens. But in India, the Central Government as well as the State Governments of Assam, West Bengal, Bihar, Delhi etc. have been willingly permitting millions of Bangladeshi Muslims to infiltrate into our country. In fact, they are conniving with these infiltrators, giving them indirect encouragement and protection, showing a keenness to give them full benefits of citizenship by issuing ration cards to them, entering their names in voters' list, and so on.

The I.S.I., the intelligence agency of Pakistan, has virtually covered the whole of India with an elaborate network of its own. Here are the intelligence activities of an enemy country penetrating our territory deeply, our own intelligence departments have reported this with concern from every affected state, but the Indian State sits practically idle to let this threat to our security thrive. The reason? The reason is that the network concerned consists of Muslims. When our Intelligence Bureau sent an officer from Bombay to Patna earlier this year to arrest a *maulvi* who was an active agent of the I.S.I., the Chief Minister of Bihar, Laloo Prasad Yadav, himself intervened to thwart the arrest. The situation in U.P. and West Bengal is no different.[5]

Over the last few years, there have been several incidents in Punjab and Jammu, in which some passengers were segregated and dragged out of buses to be lined up on the roadside and shot to death. You should remember that in each one of these incidents, the victims of the butchery, persons killed like dogs, were Hindus and Hindus alone, and they were so killed because they were Hindus. And still you think we are free?

The entire Hindu population of the Valley of Kashmir, a province of our own country, has been languishing for the last five years in makeshift tents. In the face of inhuman cruelty and terror inflicted by Muslims, these people had to leave their hearths and homes, their property and livelihood. They had to flee the homeland of their ancestors and take shelter in refugee camps. After they left, the Muslims looted and burnt their houses. During these five years, there have been three Prime Ministers in the country, but not one of them had a day's time or the decency to even visit any of these camps. Why? Because the sufferers are Hindus. The Government of India has not even stated categorically till this day that it is committed to the safe return of these

5. The subsequent events at the Nadwa College at Lucknow in November 1994 prove that the Government of India actually encourages I.S.I. activists in India. When Abu Bakr, a hard-core agent of the I.S.I. was nabbed in a raid on the College hostel which he had been using as his hideout for the last eight years to carry out terrorist and subversive activities all over India, the Government intervened swiftly and let him escape, apologized to the Rector of the College for the arrest, promised to him not to make such arrests in his institution in future, set up a high-level enquiry, and took to task the officials of the Indian Intelligence Bureau and U.P. State Police who had conducted the raid.

people to their own homes and properties.

About one lakh Hindus — Sahajdharis and Sikhs — who had fled Pakistan during the post-Partition carnage in 1947 and taken shelter in the State of Jammu & Kashmir, have not been granted state citizenship till this day. They have no right to vote in the elections to the state legislature and the panchayats, no right to get loans etc. from government institutions, no right to get their children admitted in the medical and engineering colleges of the State. Why? Because they are Hindus. The condition of 50,000 Chakma — Buddhist — refugees who had to flee East Pakistan to settle in Arunachal Pradesh, is exactly the same.

In the capital city of our country, there are still roads commemorating persons like Aurangzeb, Sikandar Lodi, Firoz Tughlaq etc. There is no conceivable tyranny that these barbarians did not practise on our national society and culture; there is no effort they spared to destroy us. They have been the worst enemies of our nation. Even their names should evoke revulsion in us. But the State in India has been glorifying them.

Muslims exploded a powerful bomb in the Madras office of the R.S.S. The explosion destroyed the building and left seven persons dead, but Rajesh Pilot, the Minister of State in the Home Ministry, Government of India, stated that the occurrence was not serious enough to warrant a C.B.I. investigation. Why? Because the R.S.S. is a Hindu organisation.

For people who openly indulge in anti-Hindu activities, incite the minorities to take to anti-national mischief, and boldly proclaim themselves to be representatives of a marauding culture, arrest warrants from Indian courts are not applicable. Warrants for the arrest of Abdullah Bukhari, Iman of Jama Masjid at Delhi, have been issued long ago by courts in Kerala, U.P., and Bihar, but the armed police force of India have not the courage to take him into custody.

In contrast, any Hindu holy man, let him be Shankaracharya Swaroopanandaji or any one else, can be arrested at any time on the slightest pretext.

Hundreds of holy sites of the Hindus, be they in Ayodhya, Mathura and Kashi, or in Ujjain, Dwaraka, Devagiri, Patan, Ajmer, Kangra, Thanesar or anywhere else, are being trampled down till this day under monuments of victory erected by alien invaders. We have not been able to liberate them. Even our right to liberate them has not been conceded by the Indian State. On the contrary, the Indian Parliament has now passed a law that attempts to liberate them would be construed as serious criminal offence.

Sanskrit, the sacred language of the Hindus, is being slowly but systematically edged out. State Governments in the country are now working to even throw it out of the school curriculum. By contrast, Urdu which is primarily the language of Muslims, which is written in a foreign script, which is the official language of Pakistan, and which had played a prominent role in fanning Muslim separatism leading to the Partition, is being blatantly encouraged. Today it is made the official language of some states, tomorrow it is recognized as a medium of examination, the day after it becomes a language of Doordarshan, and so on.

If anybody wants to run in India today a school that imparts education in Islamic or Christian theology, the Central and State Governments will be giving it grants, maybe they would even meet the entire expenses of the school on many fronts. But start a school where you want to educate your children about Hindu Dharma and culture, teaching them the Bhagvad Gita or invocations to Goddess Saraswati, the burden of funding your school will have to be shouldered by the Kalyan Ashram, or the Friends of Tribal Society, or other voluntary organizations like them. Why? Because the Government of this country will not bear costs of such a school.

The Courts in India

Have a look at our courts, the Government of India bans the Vishva Hindu Parishad and the Jamaat-i-Islami. A court decides that the ban on the former is justified but that on the latter is utterly illegal! Ferocious Muslim terrorists from India and abroad arm themselves with deadly weapons and ensconce in the Hazratbal mosque. Our courts warn our soldiers, "Beware! don't shoot at them, send them *biryāni* and chicken to eat, send them water, send them medicines." Secularism which is a synonym for anti-Hinduism has not been defined in the Constitution, but the highest court of the land passes a judgment that as such-and-such party does not support Secularism, therefore it has no right to function through State Governments. The Chief Election Commissioner issues an order for intensive revision of electoral rolls in Assam so that the rolls may be purged of names of Bangladeshi infiltrators, but the courts rule that it would be illegal to do so.[6]

The Media

Look at our national media of communication, the Doordarshan — DD. It presents as a national hero no less a villain than Tipu Sultan who demolished 8,000 Hindu temples, slaughtered Hindus in large numbers, forcibly converted thousands of them by circumcision and feeding of beef. The DD shows for months a serial styled 'The Sword of Tipu Sultan' even when that sword bears on it a carved message expressing the man's eagerness to extinguish Hinduism and eradicate the Hindu populace. That sword is still preserved in the Mysore Museum for anyone to see. Amir Khusro, a man who abused Hindus and Bhagvan Shiva in such filthy language that I cannot even repeat it before an audience which includes women, is projected by the DD as

6. Recently there have been some more judgments which display the same disposition, notably the Supreme Court judgments on Ayodhya Reference and the photo-identity cards.

a Sufi saint, a great national hero. In the 'Firdaus' programme of the DD, the terrorist Muslims of Kashmir are depicted as liberal, tolerant, and gentle people while the Hindus, the victims of their atrocities, are painted as mean and mischievous rogues.

In the major newspapers and periodicals of India, the situation today is: write whatever trash you like castigating Hindu Dharma, Hindu culture and Hindu society, let it even be utterly baseless and outright abusive, your piece will be published like a shot. But write a piece on Mohammed or Islam, let it be a factual, logical, truthful article written in decent language and based on impeccable sources, you would not be able to find space for it in any newspaper or periodical. It is as if a policy of strict Islamic censorship is operating in the country.

A Nation without A State

There is no State today, certainly not in India, to protect Hindu interests in the international arena, to raise voice for the Hindus. If Jews are unjustly treated in any part of the world, the State of Israel, representative of an independent Jewish nation, immediately raises its voice. Recently, when some Jews were killed in a bomb explosion in Argentina, the Government of Israel took less than an hour to announce that it will not spare the murderers. But what is the situation of Hindus? In December 1992, no less than 600 Hindu temples were destroyed in Bangladesh, thousands of Hindu homes were burnt down, hundreds of Hindu women were paraded naked on the streets of Bhola town, a number of Hindus were killed, Hindu shops were looted, Hindu deities were desecrated, Hindu girls were dishonoured. But the Government of India remained silent. In Pakistan, 300 temples were destroyed. In Lahore a Minister of Pakistan personally supervised the pulling down of a temple with the help of bulldozers, and several Hindus were murdered. But the Government of India remained silent. No matter how much tyranny, how much injustice is heaped on Hindus anywhere in the world, the State of India is not bothered — this is the essence of Secularism of the Indian State.

Some years ago, Sunil Wadhera, a Hindu, died in an accident in Saudi Arabia. In case of death like this, every Muslim gets a compensation of 6 to 7 lakh dinars in that country. But Wadhera's family was given only 17,000 dinars in compensation even when the insurance company had paid the normal amount. It was said that as Wadhera was a *Kāfir*, the value of his life was no more than a paltry sum. This is the Islamic law of that country. It is there. What is significant, however, is that even against such an inhuman, outrageous affront, there was no State which could raise its voice on behalf of the Hindu. Sikhs are still not granted visas to enter Saudi Arabia, because they are considered the worst *Kāfirs*.

Some of you have been to U.K. There you have seen the ISKCON temple at Watford which happens to be the biggest Hindu temple in that country and a place of assemblage for thousands of Hindus on festive occasions. The British Government is hell-bent on closing down that temple. It has issued orders to that effect. The temple will get closed any day. But there is no State, no Government in the world that would raise voice against this, or protest, or take the matter up with the British Government.

The baggage of every Hindu who lands today at the airports of Dubai, Abu Dhabi, Riyadh, Teheran etc. is searched. If it yields even a small portrait of a Hindu God or Goddess, even a tiny image of some Hindu deity, a copy of the Bhagvad Gita or Satyartha Prakash, or if the passenger is found wearing a garland of *rudrāksha* or a locket of Shri Ram, or Shiva, or Mahavirji, the objects are torn out of his neck or pulled out of his bag, broken, and consigned to the trash bin. There is no State today to protest against this national humiliation.

You may also cast a glance at the contempt with which other countries treat us. They all take us for granted. When the Foreign Minister of Israel visited India in 1991-92 and met Shri L.K. Advani, the PLO chief Yasser Arafat felt bold enough to protest against the meeting. The PLO ambassador in our country, while addressing a public meeting at Hyderabad, went to the extent of issuing a warning to the Government of India not to become too friendly to Israel. When the mosque built on the Ramajanma-bhumi site at Ayodhya was demolished in December 1992, the Government of Iran virtually issued a dictat to the Government of India that it get the mosque rebuilt at the same site. Last year, the University of Delhi invited Mr. Ismail Ahmad, Chief Justice of Namibia, to confer on him an honorary Doctorate of Law. Mr. Ahmad was not content just to receive the degree, he used his speech to castigate Hindus in strong language for demolition of the structure on the Ramajanmabhumi. The Vice-President of India, the Vice-Chancellor of the University, and several other worthies sat there and listened to him in stony silence.

How many examples of this sort should I give? Please think for yourself: are these the emblems of a free nation? Could such things happen to any independent nation? Hindus are not yet a free nation. We are still orphans, helpless, subjugated. We still don't have our own State that would work in our interest.

We have seen that the present Constitution of India is not based on Hindu ideals and ethos. Its provisions have been framed disregarding Hindu values and Hindu cultural and social traditions. It is always the preamble of a nation's constitution which proclaims what is its national identity, what are its national ideals and goals, what is its national culture, for the weal of which society has it been framed. The present Constitution of India appears to be screaming at the top of its voice to announce that the India it talks of represents neither the Hindu nation, nor the Hindu religion, nor the Hindu culture, nor the Hindu society. In it there is no place for *dharma*, no place for spirituality, or renunciation, or service, or truth, or harmony, or tolerance. By no stretch of imagination can you consider it a constitution for the Hindus, or of the Hindu nation. A constitution that ignores Hindu ideals, which gives the nation less right than to its minorities, which does not recognize Hindus as a nation, cannot be *our* constitution. In my opinion, those who regard the present Constitution of India as their own — no matter how big leaders they may be — have not yet comprehended the concept of the Hindu nation.

Quite clearly, the fundamental mistake that dogs Hindu perception today is that we are assuming Nehruvians or Secularists to be Hindus because of mere accident of their birth, and having entrusted the state power in our homeland to their hands, we are imagining that we are in a state of self-rule, that we have our country's polity in our own hands. We are assuming their state to be ours, their Constitution to be our constitution. The truth is, as I said earlier, the Secularist State and its Constitution represent only a mythical, an artificial nation styled "*Bhāratīya*" which is different from the Hindu nation and is founded on anti-Hinduism.

A Clear National Vision Needed

The sole task before us Hindus now is that we rescue ourselves from the suicidal stranglehold of the alternate nation-perception of Gandhi and Nehru, and awaken national consciousness in ourselves. We have to develop a clear national vision. Such a vision would show us that

(i) We Hindus are a nation, not a religious community. There must be a firm conviction in our minds that our national identity is Hindu. We would declare the name of our nationality to be Hindu, and no other name would be acceptable to us.

(ii) The distinctive feature of our nation is Sanātana Dharma. In its myriad forms such as Shakta, Shaiva, Sikh, Buddhist etc., it is this Dharma which gives us our national identity. We shall not accept any other ideology as the heritage of our country. We cannot regard any alien creed as our own religion.

(iii) Undivided India is our motherland. Even though parts of it have seceded today, we do not accept this division. Our goal is to re-unite the whole of our ancestral homeland into our motherland, no matter how long it takes.

(iv) Hindu culture is our national culture, Hindu society is our national society, Hindu art is our national art, Hindu literature is our national literature. Hindu history is our national history; there is no Muslim Period or British Period in this history; it is a history of continuous Hindu struggle against Muslim invaders and British colonialists. The struggle is still continuing.

(v) People subscribing the theologies of alien religions are minorities in our country, not a part of our nation. We consider these alien ideologies to be enemies of our nation. The goal is to bring our minorities back into our nation after destroying the deadly intoxication of these ideologies.

(vi) Sanskrit is our national mother-tongue, with its sister languages and many offsprings.

(vii) We are still a subjugated, enslaved nation. Nehruvian Secularists are not our own people. Their regime is not our regime. We have to liberate our motherland from their stranglehold and earn our freedom.

So far there has been an utter lack of such national consciousness or clarity of national vision amongst Hindus. The main reason for this is the failure of our intellectual awakening. We all must cultivate a habit of reading. In order to know the truth, to understand national issues, to be able to read right messages in events — we have much to read. It is extremely important that we study the alien religions, specially the Koran and Hadis and the Bible. It is also necessary for us to study Indian history in depth as well as the literature of Sanātana Dharma.

Great work is being done in this direction by some scholars in Delhi such as Ram Swarup, Sitaram Goel, Arun Shourie and others. Very high quality books are being published by these scholars under the auspices of VOICE OF INDIA. Reading these books is bound to help in arousing our national consciousness. It is my earnest request that all of you must start reading so that your national vision becomes clear. I assure you that as you start reading this well researched and thoroughly documented literature you would feel as if someone is removing blinkers from your eyes.

The Hindu National Goal

In the end, I can place the substance of my address to you by saying that there is only one task before us Hindus now: TO SECURE OUR FREEDOM. Those who say that we have to establish a Hindu nation, use wrong words; the correct words would be — THE HINDU NATION HAS TO GAIN ITS INDEPENDENCE. We have to start a new struggle for independence, the Hindu nation has to break the shackles of slavery and earn real freedom. This is our first national goal.

After securing freedom, we have to set up our own national state — A HINDU NATION-STATE. We have to discard the present Indian Constitution and give ourselves a new constitution of our own: then we have to change almost all laws and policies and replace them by enacting new ones in keeping with our national ideals and interests.

The whole world now accepts the notion of nation-states. Every nation has the right to establish, in its traditional homeland, its own state which would represent the aspirations of that nation. Even tiny little nations have now got their own states. But what an irony of fate it is that we Hindus who are one-sixth of the world's population, who are the oldest and one of the largest nations of the world, have not been able to set up our own nation-state so far. The present Indian State is an anti-nation, anti-Hindu state but, tragically, we are mistaking that very state to be our own.

Therefore, the second national goal of the Hindus is that after securing freedom, we shall set up in India a Hindu State, which will be our nation-state. It will be a state which would be founded on Hindu ideals; which will conduct its affairs in accordance with Hindu values; which would work for the all-round resurgence of the Hindus; which will protect Hindu interests not only in India but in the whole world; which will represent Hindu culture abroad; which will promote and propagate Hindu ethos in the world; which will create in our younger generations a sense of pride and self-respect in their Hindu nationality; which will not encourage feelings of division, animosity, high-and-low and we-and-they within the Hindu fold on the basis of caste; which will work for greater cohesion, harmony and collective sentiment within the Hindu society; which will not only accord the highest place to Sanātana Dharma but also protect its values, project its glory in the world, and make it its source of inspiration; which will endeavour to help Hindu art and literature to progress; which will make no slavish effort to imagine marauding cultures as our own heritage; and which will consider it its highest duty to protect Hindu honour.

Such a state we have to establish in our motherland. Swami Vivekananda had tirelessly reminded us that the glory of Sanātana Dharma gives us the inspiration and the self-confidence that we Hindus are not inferior to any nation anywhere in the world in any sense. This is what we have to prove now through our efforts, through our own nation-state — the glorious Hindu State that we are out to set up.

This, my friends, is to my mind the true and right concept of the Hindu nation; this, my friend, is our sacred duty in the days to come.

Vande Mātaram.

APPENDIX

Sri Aurobindo's Vision of Indian Nationalism[1]

On the Hindu Nation

1904 (?)

For what is a nation? What is our mother-country? It is not a piece of earth, nor a figure of speech, nor a fiction of the mind. It is a mighty Shakti, composed of the Shaktis of all the millions of units that make up the nation, just as Bhawani Mahisha Mardini sprang into being from the Shakti of all the millions of gods assembled in one mass of force and welded into unity. The Shakti we call India, Bhawani Bharati, is the living unity of the Shaktis of three hundred million people,[2] but she is inactive, imprisoned in the magic circle of Tamas, the self-indulgent inertia and ignorance of her sons....

June 19, 1907

Apart from the natural attachment which every man has to his country, its literature, it traditions, its customs and usages, patriotism has an additional stimulus in the acknowledged excellence of a national civilisation. If Britons love England with all her faults, why should we fail to love India whose faults were whittled down to an irreducible minimum till foreign conquests threw the whole society out of gear? But instead of being dominated by the natural ambition of carrying the banner of such a civilisation all over the world, we are unable to maintain its integrity in its

1. Excerpts that follow have been taken from *India's Rebirth*, Mysore, 1993.

2. When Sri Aurobindo wrote this, the population of India, which included present-day Pakistan and Bangladesh, was three hundred million.

own native home. This is betraying a trust. This is unworthiness of the worst type. We have not been able to add anything to this precious bequest; on the contrary we have been keeping ourselves and generations yet unborn from a full enjoyment of their lawful heritage....

According to Sidgwick,[3] physical expansion proceeds from a desire for spiritual expansion and history also supports the assertion. But why should not India then be the first power in the world? Who else has the undisputed right to extend spiritual sway over the world? This was Swami Vivekananda's plan of campaign. India can once more be made conscious of her greatness by an overmastering sense of the greatness of her spirituality. This sense of greatness is the main feeder of all patriotism. This only can put an end to all self-depreciation and generate a burning desire to recover the lost ground.

October 7, 1907

This great and ancient nation was once the fountain of human light, the apex of human civilisation, the examplar of courage and humanity, the perfection of good Government and settled society, the mother of all religions, the teacher of all wisdom and philosophy. It has suffered much at the hands of inferior civilisations and more savage peoples; it has gone down into the shadow of night and tasted often of the bitterness of death. Its pride has been trampled into the dust and its glory has departed. Hunger and misery and despair have become the masters of this fair soil, these noble hills, these ancient rivers, these cities whose life story goes back into prehistoric night. But do you think that therefore God has utterly abandoned us and given us

3. A writer who, defending British imperialism, spoke of "the justifible pride which the cultivated members of a civilised community feel in the beneficent exercise of dominion and in the performance by their nation of the noble task of spreading the highest kind of civilisation [*sic*!]."

up for ever to be a mere convenience for the West, the helots of its commerce, and the feeders of its luxury and pride?...

May 30, 1909

(From the famous Uttarpara Speech)

When I approached God at that time [after Sri Aurobindo's return from England], I hardly had a living faith in Him. The agnostic was in me, the atheist was in me, the sceptic was in me and I was not absolutely sure that there was a God at all. I did not feel his presence. Yet something drew me to the truth of the Vedas, the truth of the Gita, the truth of the Hindu religion.[4] I felt there must be a mighty truth somewhere in this Yoga, a mighty truth in this religion based on the Vedanta. So when I turned to the Yoga and resolved to practise it and find out if my idea was right, I did it in this spirit and with this prayer to Him, " If Thou art, then Thou knowest my heart. Thou knowest that I do not ask for Mukti, I do not ask for anything which others ask for. I ask only for strength to uplift this nation, I ask only to be allowed to live and work for this people whom I love and to whom I pray that I may devote my life." I strove long for the realisation of Yoga and at last to some extent I had it, but in what I most desired I was not satisfied. Then in the seclusion of the jail,[5] of the solitary cell I asked for it again, I said, "Give me Thy Adesh. I do not know what work to do or how to do it. Give me a message." In the communion of Yoga two messages came. The first message said, " I have given you a work and it is to help to uplift this nation. Before long the time will come when you will have to go out of jail; for it is not my will

4. It is important to note that Sri Aurobindo, in the Indian context, uses the word "religion" not in a narrow dogmatic sense, but always in the broader Hindu view of *dharma*.

5. Sri Aurobindo was in Alipore Jail, Calcutta, as an accused in a conspiracy case.

that this time either you should be convicted or that you should pass the time, as others have to do, in suffering for their country. I have called you to work, and that is the Adesh for which you have asked. I give you the Adesh to go forth and do my work." The second message came and it said, "Something has been shown to you in this year of seclusion, something about which you had your doubts and it is the truth of the Hindu religion. It is this religion that I am raising up before the world, it is this that I have perfected and developed through the Rishis, saints and Avatars, and now it is going forth to do my work among the nations. I am raising up this nation to send forth my word.... When therefore it is said that India shall rise, it is the Sanatan Dharma that shall rise. When it is said that India shall be great, it is the Sanatan Dharma that shall be great. When it is said that India shall expand and extend herself, it is the Sanatan Dharma that shall expand and extend itself over the world. It is for the Dharma and by the Dharma that India exists...."

But what is the Hindu religion? What is this religion which we call Sanatan, eternal? It is the Hindu religion only because the Hindu nation has kept it, because in this Peninsula it grew up in the seclusion of the sea and the Himalayas, because in this sacred and ancient land it was given as a charge to the Aryan race[6] to preserve through the ages. But it is not circumscribed by the confines of a single country, it does not belong peculiarly and for ever to a bounded part of the world. That which we call the Hindu religion is really the eternal religion, because it is the universal religion which embraces all others. If a religion is

---

6. Sri Aurobindo never subscribed to the theory of an Aryan invasion of India; in fact, he refuted the theory most forcefully. When he uses the expression "Aryan race", he means the Hindu nation. He never subscribed to the absurd division between Aryans and Dravidians: "I regard the so-called Aryans and Dravidians as one homogeneous race," he wrote later in *The Secret of the Veda.*

not universal, it cannot be eternal. A narrow religion, a sectarian religion, an exclusive religion can live only for a limited time and a limited purpose. This is the one religion that can triumph over materialism by including and anticipating the discoveries of science and the speculations of philosophy. It is the one religion which impresses on mankind the closeness of God to us and embraces in its compass all the possible means by which man can approach God. It is the one religion which insists every moment on the truth which all religions acknowledge that He is in all men and all things and that in Him we move and have our being. It is the one religion which enables us not only to understand and believe this truth but to realise it with every part of our being. It is the one religion which shows the world what the world is, that it is the Lila of Vasudeva. It is the one religion which shows us how we can best play our part in that Lila, its subtlest laws and its noblest rules. It is the one religion which does not separate life in any smallest detail from religion, which knows what immorality is and has utterly removed from us the reality of death....

I said [last year] that this movement is not a political movement and that nationalism is not politics but a religion, a creed, a faith. I say it again today, but I put it in another way. I say no longer that nationalism is a creed, a religion, a faith; I say that it is the Sanatan Dharma which for us is nationalism.... The Sanatan Dharma, that is nationalism. This is the message that I have to speak to you.

November 6, 1909

The Mahomedans base their separateness and their refusal to regard themselves as Indians first and Mahomedans afterwards on the existence of great Mahomedan nations to which they feel themselves more akin, in spite of our common birth and blood, than to us. Hindus have no such resource. For good or evil, they are bound to the soil and to the soil alone. They cannot deny their Mother, neither can they mutilate her. Our ideal therefore is an Indian Nationalism, largely Hindu in its spirit and traditions, because the Hindu made the land and the people and persists, by the greatness of his past, his civilisation and his culture and his invincible virility, in holding it, but wide enough also to include the Moslem and his culture and traditions and absorb them into itself.

August, 1918

when we look at the past of India, what strikes us... is her stupendous vitality, her inexhaustible power of life and joy of life, her almost unimaginably prolific creativeness. For three thousand years at least, — it is indeed much longer, — she has been creating abundantly and incessantly, lavishly, with an inexhaustible many-sidedness, republics and kingdoms and empires, philosophies and cosmogonies and sciences and creeds and arts and poems and all kinds of monuments, palaces and temples and public works, communities and societies and religious orders, laws and codes and rituals, physical sciences, psychic sciences, systems of Yoga, systems of politics and administration, arts spiritual, arts worldly, trades, industries, fine crafts, — the list is endless and in each item there is almost a plethora of activity. She creates and is not satisfied and creates and is not tired; she will not have an end of it, seems hardly to need a space for rest, a time for inertia and lying fallow. She expands too outside her borders; her ships cross the ocean and the fine superfluity of her wealth brims over to Judea and Egypt and Rome; her colonies spread her arts and epics and creeds in the Archipelago; her traces are found in the sands of Mesopotamia; her religions conquer China and Japan and spread westward as far as Palestine and Alexandria, and the figures of the Upanishads and the sayings of the Buddhists are re-echoed on the lips of Christ. Everywhere, as on her soil, so in her works there is teeming of a super-abundant energy of life....

Indeed without this opulent vitality and opulent intellectuality India could never have done so much as she did with her spiritual tendencies. It is a great error to suppose that spirituality flourishes best in an impoverished soil with the life half-killed and the intellect discouraged and intimidated. The spirituality that so flourishes is something morbid, hectic and exposed to perilous reactions. It is when the race has lived most richly and thought most profoundly that spirituality finds its heights and its depths and its constant and many-sided fruition.

May, 1919

[Hinduism] is in the first place a non-dogmatic inclusive religion and would have taken even Islam and Christianity into itself, if they had tolerated the process.

August, 1919

The religious culture which now goes by the name of Hinduism ... gave itself no name, because it set itself no sectarian limits; it claimed no universal adhesion, asserted no sole infallible dogma, set up no single narrow path or gate of salvation; it was less a creed or cult than a continuously enlarging tradition of the Godward endeavor of the human spirit. An immense many-sided and many-staged provision for a spiritual self-building and self-finding, it had some right to speak of itself by the only name it knew, the eternal religion, *sanātana dharma*...

October 19, 1935

If it is meant by the statement[7] that form of religion is something permanent and unchangeable, then it cannot be accepted. But if religion here means one's way of communion

---

7. Statement of Mahatama Gandhi in response to Dr. Ambedkar's call for mass conversion of the depressed classes to some religion other than Hinduism.

with the Divine, then it is true that that is something belonging to the inner being and cannot be changed like a house or a cloak for the sake of some personal, social or worldly convenience. If a change is to be made, it can only be for an inner spiritual reason, because of some development from within. No one can be bound to any form of religion or any particular creed or system, but if he changes the one he has accepted for another, for external reasons, that means he has inwardly no religion at all and both his old and his new religion are only an empty formula. At bottom that is I suppose what the statement drives at. Preference for a different approach to the Truth or the desire of inner spiritual self-expression are not the motives of the recommendation of change to which objection is made by the Mahatma here; the object proposed [by Dr. Ambedkar] is an enhancement of social status and consideration which is no more a spiritual motive than conversion for the sake of money or marriage. If a man has no religion in himself, he can change his credal profession for any motive; if he has, he cannot; he can only change it in response to an inner spiritual need. If a man has a bhakti for the Divine in the form of Krishna, he can't very well say, "I will swap Krishna for Christ so that I may become socially respectable."

September 19, 1936

Religion is always imperfect because it is a mixture of man's spirituality with his endeavours that come in in trying to sublimate ignorantly his lower nature. Hindu religion appears to me as a cathedral-temple, half in ruins, noble in the mass, often fantastic in detail but always fantastic with a significance — crumbling or badly outworn in places, but a cathedral-temple in which service is still done to the Unseen and its real presence can be felt by those who enter with the right spirit. The outer social structure which it built for its approach is another matter.

On the Muslim Problem

September 13, 1906

The idea that the election of a Mahomedan President will conciliate the anti-Congress Mahomedans is a futility which has been repeatedly exposed by experience.

June 19, 1909

We do not fear Mahomedan opposition; so long as it is the honest Swadeshi article and not manufactured in Shillong or Simla,[8] we welcome it as a sign of life and aspiration. We do not shun, we desire the awakening of Islam in India even if its first crude efforts are misdirected against ourselves; for all strength, all energy, all action is grist to the mill of the nation-builder. In that faith we are ready, when the time comes for us to meet in the political field, to exchange with the Mussulman, just as he chooses, the firm clasp of the brother or the resolute grip of the wrestler....

Of one thing we may be certain, that Hindu-Mahomedan unity cannot be effected by political adjustments or Congress flatteries. It must be sought deeper down, in the heart and in the mind, for where the causes of disunion are, there the remedies must be sought. We shall do well in trying to solve the problem to remember that misunderstanding is the most fruitful cause of our differences, that love compels love and that strength conciliates the strong. We must strive to remove the causes of misunderstanding by a better mutual knowledge and sympathy; we must extend the unfaltering love of the patriot to our Mussulman brother, remembering always that in him too Narayana dwells and to him too our Mother has given a permanent place in her bosom; but we must cease to approach him falsely or flatter out of a selfish weakness and cowardice. We believe this to be the only practical way of dealing with the difficulty. As a political

---

8. Seats of the British colonial government in India.

question the Hindu-Mahomedan problem does not interest us at all, as a national problem it is of supreme importance.

September 4, 1909

Every action for instance which may be objectionable to a number of Mahomedans is now liable to be forbidden because it is likely to lead to a breach of the peace, and one is dimly beginning to wonder whether the day may not come when worship in Hindu temples may be forbidden on that valid ground.

November 20, 1909

...Formerly, there were only two classes in India, the superior European and the inferior Indian; now there will be three, the superior European, the superior Mahomedan and the inferior Hindu....

April 18, 1923

I am sorry they are making a fetish of this Hindu-Muslim unity.[9] It is no use ignoring facts; some day the Hindus may have to fight the Muslims and they must prepare for it. Hindu-Muslim unity should not mean the subjection of the Hindus. Every time the mildness of the Hindu has given way. The best solution would be to allow the Hindus to organize themselves and the Hindu-Muslim unity would take care of itself, it would automatically solve the problem. Otherwise, we are lulled into a false sense of satisfaction that we have solved a difficult problem, when in fact we have only shelved it.

July 23, 1923

You can live amicably with a religion whose principle is toleration. But how is it possible to live peacefully with a religion whose principle is "I will not tolerate you"? How are you going to have unity with these people? Certainly,

9. Sri Aurobindo's comments on the largscale Hindu-Muslim riots that followed the short-lived Khilafat agitation of 1920-22.

Hindu-Muslim unity cannot be arrived at on the basis that the Muslims will go on converting Hindus while the Hindus shall not convert any Mahomedan. *You can't build unity on such basis. Perhaps the only way of making the Mohammedans harmless is to make them lose their religion.*[10]

September 12, 1923

The Mahomedan or Islamic culture hardly gave anything to the world which may be said to be of fundamental importance and typically its own; Islamic culture was mainly borrowed from others. Their mathematics and astronomy and other subjects were derived from India and Greece. It is true they gave some of these things a new turn, but they have not created much. Their philosophy and their religion are very simple and what they call Sufism is largely the result of gnostics who lived in Persia and it is the logical outcome of that school of thought largely touched by Vedanta.

I have, however, mentioned [in *The Foundations of Indian Culture*] that Islamic culture contributed the Indo-Saracenic architecture to Indian culture. I do not think it has done anything more in India of cultural value. It gave some new forms to art and poetry. Its political institutions were always semi-barbaric.

May 18, 1926

Look at Indian politicians: all ideas, ideas — they are busy with ideas. Take the Hindu-Muslim problem: I don't know why our politicians accepted Gandhi's Khilafat agitation.[11]

---

10. The two italicised lines at the end of this passage have been restored with reference to the full statement as found in *Evening Talks with Sri Aurobindo* by A.B. Purani, Second Series, Pondicherry, 1974, p. 48.

11. From the outset Mahatma Gandhi made it clear that the Khilafat question was in his view more important and urgent than that of Swaraj. He wrote: "To the Musalmans, Swaraj means, as it must, India's ability to deal effectively with the Khilafat question... It is impossible not to sympathise with this attitude... I would gladly ask for postponement of Swaraj activity if thereby we could advance the interest of the Khilafat."

With the mentality of the ordinary Mahomedan it was bound to produce the reaction it has produced: you fed the force, it gathered power and began to make demands which the Hindu mentality had to rise up and reject. That does not require Supermind to find out, it requires common sense. Then, the Mahomedan reality and the Hindu reality began to break heads at Calcutta.[12] The leaders are busy trying to square the realities with their mental ideas instead of facing them straight....

June 29, 1926

If it is India's destiny to assimilate all the conflicting elements, is it possible to assimilate the Mahomedan element also?

Why not? India has assimilated elements from the Greeks, the Persians and other nations. But she assimilates only when her central truth is recognized by the other party, and even while assimilating she does it in such a way that the elements absorbed are no longer recognizable as foreign but become part of herself. For instance, we took from the Greek architecture, from the Persian painting, etc.

The assimilation of the Mahomedan culture also was done in the mind to a great extent and it would have perhaps gone further. But in order that the process may be complete it is necessary that a change in the Mahomedan mentality should come. The conflict is in the outer life and unless the Mahomedans learn tolerance I do not think the assimilation is possible.

The Hindu is ready to tolerate. He is open to new ideas and his culture has got a wonderful capacity for assimilation, but always provided that India's central truth is recognized.

August 1, 1926

The attempt to placate the Mahomedans was a false diplomacy. Instead of trying to achieve Hindu-Muslim unity

12. A reference to serious riots in Calcutta the previous month.

directly, if the Hindus had devoted themselves to national work, the Mahomedans would have gradually come of themselves.... This attempt to patch up a unity has given too much importance to the Muslims and it has been the root of all these troubles.

Undated (1934)

As for the Hindu-Muslim affair, I saw no reason why the greatness of India's past or her spirituality should be thrown into the waste paper basket in order to conciliate the Moslems who would not at all be conciliated by such policy. What has created the Hindu-Moslem split was not Swadeshi, but the acceptance of the communal principle by the Congress (here Tilak made his great blunder), and the further attempt by the Khilafat movement to conciliate them and bring them in on wrong lines. The recognition of that communal principle at Lucknow[13] made them permanently a separate political entity in India which ought never to have happened; the Khilafat affair made that separate political entity an organised separate political power.

December 30, 1939

(A disciple:) There are some people who object to "Vande Mataram" as a national song. And some Congressmen support the removal of some parts of the song.

In that case the Hindus should give up their culture.

The argument is that the song speaks of Hindu gods, like Durga, and that is offensive to the Muslims.

But it is not a religious song: it is a national song and the Durga spoken of is India as the Mother. Why should not

---

13. The reference is to the Lucknow Pact between the Indian National Congress and the Muslim League, signed in 1916. It conceded the Muslim demand for separate electorates and weightages in Legislative Councils. Lokamanya Tilak had signed it on behalf of the Congress.

the Muslims accept it? It is an image used in poetry. In the Indian conception of nationality, the Hindu view would naturally be there. If it cannot find a place there, the Hindus may as well be asked to give up their culture. The Hindus don't object to "Allah-ho-Akbar"....

Why should not the Hindu worship his god? Otherwise, the Hindus must either accept Mohammedanism or the European culture or become atheists...

I told C.R. Das [in 1932] that this Hindu-Muslim question must be solved before the Britishers go, otherwise there was a danger of civil war. He also agreed and wanted to solve it...

Instead of doing what was necessary the Congress is trying to flirt with Jinnah, and Jinnah simply thinks that he has to obstinately stick to his terms to get them. The more they try, the more Jinnah becomes intransigent.

May 28, 1940

Have you read what Gandhi has said in answer to a correspondent? He says that if eight crores of Muslims demand a separate State, what else are the twenty-five crores of Hindus to do but surrender? Otherwise there will be civil war.

> *(A disciple:) I hope that is not the type of conciliation he is thinking of.*

Not thinking of it, you say? He has actually said that and almost yielded. If you yield to the opposite party beforehand, naturally they will stick strongly to their claims. It means that the minority will rule and the majority must submit. The minority is allowed its say, " We shall be the ruler and you our servants. Our *harf* [word] will be law; you will have to obey." This shows a peculiar mind. I think this kind of people are a little cracked.

June 21, 1940

In Kashmir, the Hindus had all the monopoly. Now if the Muslim demands are acceded to, the Hindus will be wiped out.

October 7, 1940

(A disciple:) It is because of the British divide-and-rule policy that we can't unite.

Nonsense! Was there unity in India before the British rule?

But now since our national consciousness is more developed there is more chance of unity if the British don't bolster up Jinnah and his Muslim claims.

Does Jinnah want unity?... What he wants is independence for Muslims and if possible rule over India. That is the old spirit... But why is it expected that Muslims will be so accommodating? Everywhere minorities are claiming their rights. Of course, there may be some Muslims who are different, more nationalistic in outlook: even Azad has his own terms, only he sees Indian unity first and will settle those terms afterwards.

October 19, 1946

(From a letter to a disciple who expressed anguish at the widespread horrors perpetrated on Hindus by Muslims in Bengal, notably in Noakhali and Tippera districts, now in Bangladesh; this organized violence — which the British government did nothing to stop — was part of Jinnah's plan of "Direct Action" which was intended to demonstrate the impossibility for Hindus and Muslims to live together, and therefore the inevitability of Pakistan.)

As regards Bengal, things are certainly very bad; the conditions of the Hindus there are terrible and they may even get worse in spite of the Interim *mariage de convenance* at Delhi.[14] ...What is happening did not come to me as a

14. A reference to the Interim Government worked out between the British and the Congress, which the Muslim League had just agreed to join.

surprise. I foresaw it when I was in Bengal and warned people that it was probable and almost inevitable and that they should be prepared for it. At that time no one attached any value to what I said although some afterwards remembered and admitted, when the trouble first began, that I have been right; only C.R. Das had apprehensions and he even told me when he came to Pondicherry that he would not like the British to go out until this dangerous problem had been settled. But I have not been discouraged by what is happening, because I know and have experienced hundreds of times that beyond the blackest darkness there lies for one who is a divine instrument the light of God's victory. I have never had a strong and persistent will for anything to happen in the world — I am not speaking of personal things — which did not eventually happen even after delay, defeat or even disaster. There was a time when Hitler was victorious everywhere and it seemed certain that a black yoke of the Asura would be imposed on the whole world; but where is Hitler now and where is his rule? Berlin and Nuremberg have marked the end of that dreadful chapter in human history. Other blacknesses threaten to overshadow or even engulf mankind, but they too will end as that nightmare has ended.

August 15, 1947

India is free but she has not achieved unity, only a fissured and broken freedom... The old communal division into Hindu and Muslim seems to have hardened into the figure of a permanent political division of the country. It is to be hoped that the Congress and the nation will not accept the settled fact as for ever settled or as anything more than a temporary expedient. For if it lasts, India may be seriously weakened, even crippled: civil strife may remain always possible, possible even a new invasion and foreign conquest. The partition of the country must go, — it is to be hoped by a slackening of tension, by a progressive understanding of the need of peace and concord, by the constant necessity of common and concerted action, even of an instrument of union for that purpose. In this way unity may come about under whatever form — the exact form may have a pragmatic but not a fundamental importance. But by whatever means, the division must and will go. For without it the density of India might be seriously impaired and even frustrated. But that must not be.[15]

1947 (?)

The idea of two nationalities in India is only a newly-fangled notion invented by Jinnah for his purposes and contrary to the facts. More than 90% of the Indian Mussalmans are descendants of converted Hindus and belong as much to the Indian nation as the Hindus themselves. This process of conversion has continued all along; Jinnah is himself a descendant of a Hindu, converted in fairly recent times, named Jinahbhai and many of the most famous Mohammedan leaders have a similar origin.

•

On India's Future

July 13, 1911

Be very careful to follow my instructions in avoiding the old kind of politics. Spirituality is India's only politics, the fulfilment of the Sanatan Dharma its only Swaraj. I have no doubt we shall have to go through our Parliamentary period in order to get rid of the notion of Western

15. Newly created Pakistan invaded Kashmir two months later. The Indian army was able to repulse the attack and was about to drive Pakistani forces out of Kashmir when Nehru called a halt to the fighting and brought the "dispute" before the United Nations — with the result that Kashmir is still today divided and its Pakistan-occupied part a continual source of terrorism flowing into India, as part of the preparation for what Pakistani leaders have called "the need for a second partition of India."

democracy by seeing in practice how helpless it is to make nations blessed. India is passing really through the first stages of a sort of national Yoga. It was mastered in the inception by the inrush of divine force which came in 1905 and aroused it from its state of complete tamasic *ajñānam* [ignorance]. But, as happens also with individuals, all that was evil, all the wrong *samskāras* [imprints] and wrong emotions and mental and moral habits rose with it and misused the divine force. Hence all that orgy of political oratory, democratic fervour, meetings, processions, passive resistance, all ending in bombs, revolvers and Coercion laws.... God has struck it all down, — Moderatism, the bastard child of English Liberalism; Nationalism, the mixed progeny of Europe and Asia; Terrorism, the abortive offspring of Bakunin and Mazzini.... It is only when this foolishness is done with that truth will have a chance, the sattwic mind in India emerge and a really strong spiritual movement begin as a prelude to India's regeneration. No doubt, there will be plenty of trouble and error still to face, but we shall have a chance of putting our feet on the right path. In all I believe God to be guiding us, giving the necessary experiences, preparing the necessary conditions.

December, 1918

A political Europeanisation would be followed by a social turn of the same kind and bring a cultural and spiritual death in its train... Either India will be rationalised and industrialised out of all recognition and she will be no longer India or else she will be the leader in a new world-phase, aid by her example and cultural infiltration the new tendencies of the West and spiritualise the human race. That is the one radical and poignant question at issue. Will the spiritual motive which India represents prevail on Europe and create there new forms congenial to the West, or will European rationalism and commercialism put an end for ever to the Indian type of culture?

April, 1920

I believe that the main cause of India's weakness is not subjection, nor poverty, nor a lack of spirituality or Dharma, but a diminution of thought-power, the spread of ignorance in the motherland of Knowledge. Everywhere I see an inability or unwillingness to think — incapacity of thought or "thought phobia". Whatever may have been in the mediaeval period, now this attitude is the sign of a great decline. The mediaeval period was a night, a time of victory for the man of ignorance; the modern world is a time of victory for the man of knowledge. It is the one who can fathom and learn the truth of the world by thinking more, searching more, labouring more, who will gain more Shakti. Look at Europe, and you will see two things: a wide limitless sea of thought and the play of a huge and rapid, yet disciplined force. The whole Shakti of Europe lies there. It is by virtue of this Shakti that she has been able to swallow the world, like our Tapaswins of old, whose might held even the gods of the universe in awe, suspense and subjection....

August 8, 1926

The Greeks had more light than the Christians who converted them; at that time there was gnosticism in Greece, and they were developing agnosticism and so forth. The Christians brought darkness rather than light.

That has always been the case with aggressive religions — they tend to overrun the earth. Hinduism on the other hand is passive and therein lies its danger...

September 16, 1935

(A disciple:) It is rather depressing to hear about the atrocities committed by some Mahomedans on Hindu families in Bengal. With the coming of Independence

I hope such things will stop... In your scheme of things do you definitely see a free India?...

That is all settled. It is a question of working out only. The question is what is India going to do with her Independence? The above kind of affair? Bolshevism? Goonda-raj? Things look ominous.

December, 1948

India, shut into a separate existence by the Himalayas and the ocean, has always been the home of a peculiar people with characteristics of its own recognisably distinct from all others, with its own distinct civilisation, way of life, way of the spirit, a separate culture, arts, building of society. It has absorbed all that has entered into it, put upon all the Indian stamp, welded the most diverse elements into its fundamental unity. But it has also been throughout a congeries of diverse peoples, lands, kingdoms and, in earlier times, republics also, diverse races, sub-nations with a marked character of their own, developing different brands or forms of civilisation and culture, many schools of art and architecture which yet succeeded in fitting into the general Indian type of civilisation and culture. India's history throughout has been marked by a tendency, a constant effort to unite all this diversity of elements into a single political whole under a central imperial rule so that India might be politically as well as culturally one. Even after a rift had been created by the irruption of the Mohammedan peoples with their very different religion and social structure, there continued a constant effort of political unification and there was a tendency towards a mingling of cultures and their mutual influence on each other; even some heroic attempts were made to discover or create a common religion built out of these two apparently irreconcilable faiths and here too there were mutual influences....

In this hour, in the second year of its liberation the

nation has to awaken to many more very considerable problems, to vast possibilities opening before her but also to dangers and difficulties that may, if not wisely dealt with, become formidable.... There are deeper issues for India herself, since by following certain tempting directions she may conceivably become a nation like many others evolving an opulent industry and commerce, a powerful organisation of social and political life, an immense military strength, practising power-politics with a high degree of success, guarding and extending zealously her gains and her interests, dominating even a large part of the world, but in this apparently magnificent progression forfeiting its Swadharma, losing its soul. Then ancient India and her spirit might disappear altogether and we would have only one more nation like others and that would be a real gain neither to the world nor to us. There is a question whether she may prosper more harmlessly in the outward life yet lose altogether her richly massed and firmly held spiritual experience and knowledge. It would be a tragic irony of fate if India were to throw away her spiritual heritage at the very moment when in the rest of the world there is more and more a turning towards her for spiritual help and a saving Light. This must not and will surely not happen; but it cannot be said that the danger is not there. There are indeed other numerous and difficult problems that face this country or will very soon face it. No doubt we will win through, but we must not disguise from ourselves the fact that after these long years of subjection and its cramping and impairing effects a great inner as well as outer liberation and change, a vast inner and outer progress is needed if we are to fulfil India's true destiny.

Shri Abhas Chatterjee starts by clearing some prevalent misconceptions, namely, that the word "Hindu" is a geographical concept, that our national identity is *"Bhāratīya"*, that people who have been converted to alien and inimical ideologies are "nationals", that India's culture is "composite", and that we are "a nation in the making".

Next, he takes into account all available criteria—geography, history, culture, language, literature, art, spiritual tradition—regarding the definition of a nation, and draws the following firm conclusions:

- ❑ We Hindus are a Nation, not a religious community. Our national identity is Hindu not *Bhāratīya.*
- ❑ The distinctive feature of our nationhood is Sanātana Dharma. Alien and inimical ideologies like Islam, Christianity and Nehruvian Secularism are not parts of our heritage.
- ❑ Undivided India is our ancestral homeland. We do not accept its division into India, Pakistan and Bangladesh. Our goal is to re-unite the whole of our ancestral homeland, no matter how long it takes.
- ❑ Hindu culture is our national culture, Hindu society our national society, Hindu literature our national literature and Hindu art our national art.
- ❑ Hindu history is our national history. We recognize no Muslim or British period in our history. These are periods of national struggle against Islamic invaders and British colonialists. The struggle is still continuing.
- ❑ People subscribing to alien and inimical ideologies are minorities in our country, not nationals like Hindus. Our goal is to bring back the minorities into the national mainstream by liquidating the ideologies that have alienated our own people from us.
- ❑ Sanskrit is our national language along with its sister languages and all it offsprings.
- ❑ We Hindus are still a subjugated nation, enslaved and discriminated against by the regime subscribing to Nehruvian Secularism. We have to liberate our motherland from this alien stranglehold, earn our freedom, and establish our own nation-state.

What the Hindus need most at present is an intellectual and cultural awakening. Hindus have to see with their own eyes not only themselves but also the alien ideologies which have been tormenting them for several centuries.

ISBN 978-81-85990-33-0

Rs.95
₹100/.00

VOICE OF INDIA
New Delhi

MCQs in MEDICINE

with Explanations for Dental Students (BDS) and Dental PG Entrance Examinations

Shaleen Chandra
Professor & Head of the Deptt.
Saraswati Postgraduate Dental College and Hospital
233 Tiwariganj, Faizabad Road, Juggour, Lucknow
Ex- Professor & Head of the Deptt.
Sardar Patel Postgraduate Institute of Dental and Medical Sciences, Lucknow
Ex-Assistant Professor, Rama Postgraduate Dental College and Hospital and Research Centre, Kanpur
Ex-Lecturer, CSM Medical University, (Formerly KG Medical College, KG Medical University and UP KG University of Dental Sciences) Lucknow
Ex-Lecturer, Budha Postgraduate Institute of Dental Sciences, Kankar Bagh, Patna
Paper setter and Examiner of BDS, MDS and PGDE Examinations in many Universities

Satish Chandra
Best Teacher Awardee
Ex- Member, Dental Council of India
Director and Professor
Sardar Patel Postgraduate Institute of Dental and Medical Sciences, Lucknow
Ex-Professor and Head of the Department and Dean
Dental Faculty, CSM Medical University (Formerly KG Medical College, KG Medical University and UP KG University of Dental Sciences) Lucknow
Ex-Professor, Dean, Head and Principal
DJ Postgraduate College of Dental Sciences and Research, Modinagar
Ex-Professor, Dean, Head and Principal, Postgraduate Institute of Dental Sciences, Bareilly
Paper setter and Examiner for BDS, MDS and PGDE Examinations in many Universities

Girish Chandra
Director, Rajendra Nagar Hospital, Lucknow

Sourabh Chandra
Ex- Chief Resident CSM Medical University
(Formerly K.G. Medical College) K.G Medical University, Lucknow
Director, Rajendra Nagar Hospital, Lucknow

JAYPEE BROTHERS MEDICAL PUBLISHERS (P) LTD
New Delhi • Panama City • London

Published by

Jaypee Brothers Medical Publishers (P) Ltd

Corporate Office

4838/24, Ansari Road, Daryaganj, **New Delhi** 110 002, India
Phone: +91-11-43574357, Fax: +91-11-43574314
Website: www.jaypeebrothers.com

Offices in India

- **Ahmedabad**, e-mail: ahmedabad@jaypeebrothers.com
- **Bengaluru**, e-mail: bangalore@jaypeebrothers.com
- **Chennai**, e-mail: chennai@jaypeebrothers.com
- **Delhi**, e-mail: jaypee@jaypeebrothers.com
- **Hyderabad**, e-mail: hyderabad@jaypeebrothers.com
- **Kochi**, e-mail: kochi@jaypeebrothers.com
- **Kolkata**, e-mail: kolkata@jaypeebrothers.com
- **Lucknow**, e-mail: lucknow@jaypeebrothers.com
- **Mumbai**, e-mail: mumbai@jaypeebrothers.com
- **Nagpur**, e-mail: nagpur@jaypeebrothers.com

Overseas Offices

- **Central America Office, Panama City, Panama**, Ph: 001-507-317-0160
  e-mail: cservice@jphmedical.com, Website: www.jphmedical.com
- **Europe Office, UK**, Ph: +44 (0) 2031708910
  e-mail: info@jpmedpub.com

MCQs in MEDICINE

(with Explanations for Dental Students (BDS) and Dental PG Entrance Examinations)

First Edition : **2011**

ISBN 978-93-5025-419-6

Typeset at JPBMP typesetting unit

Printed in India